The Prophets

Messengers of God's Mercy

Study Set

Sarah Christmyer & Thomas Smith

West Chester, Pennsylvania

Nihil obstat: Rev. Msgr. J. Brian Bransfield, S.T.D.
Censor Librorum
December 9, 2014

Imprimatur: +Most Reverend Charles J. Chaput, O.F.M. Cap.
Archbishop of Philadelphia
December 12, 2014

The Prophets: Messengers of God's Mercy is a resource of *The Great Adventure* Catholic Bible Study Program.

Jeff Cavins, general editor, *The Great Adventure* Catholic Bible Study Program
Thomas Smith, co-author and presenter, *The Prophets: Messengers of God's Mercy*
Sarah Christmyer, editor, *The Great Adventure* and co-author, *The Prophets: Messengers of God's Mercy*
Deborah Holiday, editorial consultant, *The Prophets: Messengers of God's Mercy*

Ascension Press
Post Office Box 1990
West Chester, PA 19380
1-800-376-0520
AscensionPress.com
BibleStudyForCatholics.com

Printed in the United States of America

ISBN: 978-1-935940-70-8

THE PROPHETS

Messengers of God's Mercy

Questions

Responses

Note: *The Prophets: Messengers of God's Mercy,* like other *Great Adventure* Bible studies, quotes from and references the Revised Standard Version–Catholic Edition (RSV-CE) of the Bible. References to the *Catechism of the Catholic Church* are noted by the abbreviation "CCC," followed by the paragraph number.

[1] The "Divided Kingdom," "Exile," and "Return" in this study refer to time periods in The Great Adventure Bible Timeline learning system.

Welcome to *The Great Adventure*

*"To fall in love with God is the greatest of all romances;
to seek him, the greatest adventure."*

– St. Augustine

The Bible is at the heart of our Catholic Faith—and our relationship with God. It is the living Word of God, where our Father meets with us and lovingly speaks to us. Reading the Bible should bring us closer to Christ, but understanding it is not always easy. Many people tell us they have tried time and again to prayerfully read Scripture, but they get frustrated because they "just don't get it."

The Great Adventure is designed so that anyone can make sense of the Bible and experience the life-changing power of God's Word. At the core of *The Great Adventure* is the concept that there is a story running through the seventy-three books of the Bible that ties all of Scripture together and makes sense not just of the Bible, but of our lives as well.

That story is God's plan as it has unfolded throughout salvation history and continues to unfold today. Once we grasp this "big picture," the readings at Mass begin to make more sense, our Scripture reading and study come to life, and we see how our lives fit into God's loving plan.

Hundreds of thousands of participants have discovered the riches of Scripture by experiencing one or more *Great Adventure* Bible studies. It is our prayer that you will gain a newfound understanding of God's Word that will transform your life and bring you closer to Christ.

Jeff Cavins, Creator & President, *The Great Adventure*
Sarah Christmyer, Co-developer & Author, *The Great Adventure*

About *The Great Adventure* Catholic Bible Study Program

At the core of *The Great Adventure* is *The Bible Timeline* Learning System: a simple way to get the "big picture" of the Bible by focusing on the story that runs throughout Sacred Scripture. *Great Adventure* Bible studies explore the biblical narrative in light of Catholic teaching and the historical, cultural, and literary context of the Scriptures to discover what Scripture reveals about God's plan and our place within it. Studies of individual books of the Bible are supplemented by thematic and "life application" studies.

Every *Great Adventure* study is designed to foster:

- Familiarity with the Bible and ease of reading it
- Bible study habits consistent with the guidelines of the Catholic Church
- Personal engagement in the Word of God
- Faith-sharing based on the Word of God
- Growth in knowledge about Scripture and the Catholic Faith

About *The Prophets: Messengers of God's Mercy*

The Prophets: Messengers of God's Mercy is a powerful Bible study that will draw you closer to Christ. The prophets afflict the comfortable and comfort the afflicted, calling us to return to our covenant relationship with God. They urge us to repentance, warn us of the dangers of sin, and announce the blessings of faithfulness. Their prophetic words speak to us even today, as they draw us closer to our heavenly Bridegroom and show us how to share him with others.

Materials

Materials for *The Prophets: Messengers of God's Mercy* include:

- **Study Set.** Contains engaging study questions (with session summaries, home reading assignments, charts, and diagrams), Talk Notes, responses to the questions, and *The Bible Timeline* Chart. *(You will need one copy for every participant, study leader, and small-group facilitator.)*
- **Video Presentations** (ten, 30-minute sessions). Presented by Thomas Smith, these ten video presentations provide comprehensive teaching and commentary on the prophets. *(You will need one DVD Set.)*

In addition, every participant, leader, and small-group facilitator should have a Catholic Bible. We recommend the Revised Standard Version–Catholic Edition (RSV-CE) or the New American Bible (NAB).

How the Study Works

Every *Great Adventure* study includes four essential steps, which are designed to fit together and build upon each other. Following these steps in order will help you to get the most out of each session.

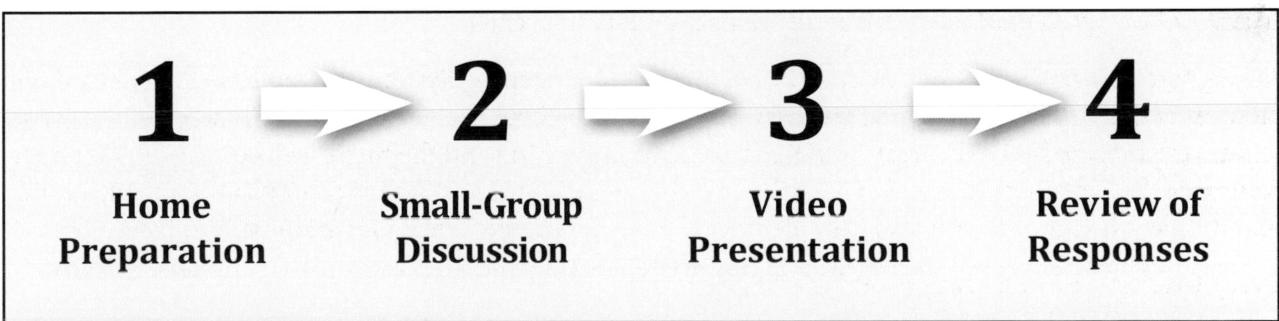

Step 1: Home Preparation

Note: There is no home preparation required for Session 1.

Each session begins with personal study that involves reading Scripture and answering a series of questions that will help you understand and think more deeply about what you have read. Some questions will include additional reading from other parts of the Bible or from the *Catechism of the Catholic Church* to help you consider the passage in light of the bigger picture of salvation history and Catholic teaching.

We recommend that you allow at least 90 minutes to complete the reading and answer the questions for each session. We also suggest that home preparation be done in several sittings over the course of a week. This will help you create a habit of daily Bible reading and prayerful meditation.

Step 2: Small-Group Discussion

The small-group discussion is one of the most effective components of a *Great Adventure* Bible study. During this discussion, members of your small group will have an opportunity to share their insights into the Scripture reading. The goal of the small-group discussion is to help participants obtain a richer understanding of the readings and apply them to their lives. Trained facilitators guide the small-group discussion and keep it on track. To learn how to facilitate a small-group discussion, visit BibleStudyForCatholics.com/Facilitators. Be sure to follow the "Ten Commandments of Small-Group Discussion" on page ix.

Step 3: Video Presentation

Thomas Smith wraps up each session with a video presentation that offers unique insights and profound connections to help you gain a deeper understanding of the Bible and its relationship to the Catholic Faith, with a special emphasis on ways to apply what you have learned to your life.

Step 4: Review of Responses

The final step—reviewing the responses at the back of this Study Set—is done at home prior to beginning the reading for the next session. These responses will help you read the Scripture passages for the next session in the proper context.

For the most effective study experience, complete these steps in the following order: (1) Read and answer the questions; (2) discuss them in your small group; (3) view the video presentation; and (4) review the responses. During discussion, your small-group facilitator will incorporate points found in the responses, but the richness that comes from individual insights can be lost when participants view the responses prior to the discussion.

For more information about how to plan and promote a Bible study and how to facilitate a small-group discussion, visit **BibleStudyForCatholics.com/Leaders,** or call our Study Consultants at 1-800-376-0520.

Session Outline and Reading Guide

Each session in this Study Set has the following sections. (Note: Session 1, does not have study questions or responses).

1. Session Questions (used during **Step 1: Home Preparation** and **Step 2: Small-Group Discussion**)

A. Establish the Context

B. Read the Story

C. Take a Deeper Look

D. Application

2. Session Talk Notes (used during **Step 3: Video Presentation**)

3. Session Responses (used during **Step 4: Review of Responses**)

The following chart offers an overview of the **home preparation** readings assigned in each session of the study. The main reading is provided in section **B. Read the Story** and should be read before you answer the study questions. Additional Bible readings and *Catechism* readings are provided in section **C. Take a Deeper Look** and should be read as you answer the study questions for each session.

Session	Main Reading	Additional Bible Readings	*Catechism* Readings (CCC)
Session 1 – Introduction to the Prophets	(None)	(None)	(None)
Session 2 – Hosea: Living God's Love Story	Hosea 1:1–4:10, 1:11, 1:14 **Going Deeper** (optional): Hosea	Matthew 9:10-13	211, 218, 2787
Session 3 – Jonah: God's Reluctant Messenger	Jonah	Genesis 3:8, 4:16; Psalm 139:1-12; Jeremiah 18:7-8; Matthew 12:38-42	(None)
Session 4 – Isaiah, Part 1: Prophet of Woe	Isaiah 1–12, 36–39 **Going Deeper (optional):** Isaiah 1–39; 2 Kings 16–20	Revelation 4:1-8	208, 2100
Session 5 – Isaiah Part 2: Prophet of Consolation	Isaiah 40, 42, 44–45, 63–66 **Going Deeper (optional):** Isaiah 40–66	Matthew 27:12-14; John 1:29; Acts 8:30-38; Romans 5:8; 1 Peter 2:23-25; Revelation 21:1-5	(None)
Session 6 – Jeremiah: The Broken-Hearted Prophet	2 Kings 22–24; Jeremiah 1–2, 7, 29:1-14, 31–33 **Going Deeper (optional):** Jeremiah	2 Kings 25:1-12; Isaiah 44:1-2, 49:1-6; Galatians 1:15-16; Matthew 21:12-13; Luke 22:19-20	584, 613, 781, 1965
Session 7 – Ezekiel: God's Watchman on the Wall	Ezekiel 1–3, 11:14-25, 34, 43:1-17, 47:1-12 **Going Deeper (optional):** Ezekiel	Isaiah 6:1-4; John 6:51-58, 10:11-18	754, 736, 1296, 1432
Session 8 – Daniel: Faithful to the End	Daniel 1–7, 9, 12 **Going Deeper (optional):** Daniel	Psalm 118:22; Isaiah 8:13-15, 28:16; Matthew 17:12, 17:22-23, 21:42-44, 24:30, 25:31-32; Acts 4:11-12; 1 Peter 2:6-8	203
Session 9 – Haggai and Malachi: Messengers of Hope	Haggai 1–2; Malachi 1–4 **Going Deeper (optional):** Ezra; Nehemiah	Deuteronomy 28:1-6, 15-19; Luke 1:8-17; James 4:6-9	(None)

Session 10 – New Testament and Modern Prophets: Messengers of the New Covenant	(None)	Deuteronomy 18:15, 18:18-19; Joel 2:28-29; Matthew 1:18-23, 2:1-6, 2:13-15, 4:12-26, 8:14-17, 13:34-35, 21:1-5; Luke 3:1-18; John 3:16, 6:14, 8:26, 8:28; Acts 1:8, 2:1-18, 3:20-26, 8:25, 8:34-35, 11:27-28, 15:22-27, 15:32; 1 Corinthians 14:1-4; Colossians 1:19-20; Hebrews 1:1-13, 2:1-3	799–801, 905

What to Do for Each Session

1. Welcome and Introduction (10 minutes)
2. Small-Group Discussion (40 minutes)
3. ***Note to Study Leaders:*** There is no small-group discussion for the first week. Instead, use this time to divide participants into small groups of eight to twelve persons, ensure that everyone has the study materials, and explain how the study works. Each small group should be led by a trained facilitator.
4. Video Presentation (30 minutes)
5. Closing and Prayer (5 minutes)

Getting the Most Out of This Study

This study will help you understand the prophets in a new way. The "head knowledge" you gain will help you grow in "heart knowledge" as you follow up on what you have learned. The Bible will always remain a mystery, though, and that is part of the beauty of it: We can never exhaust the treasures of Scripture. Fortunately for us, the Bible is not a subject to master; it is a place to encounter the living Word of God.

Whenever you open your Bible to read, *start with prayer,* and place yourself in God's presence. You might take Samuel's prayer as your own: "Speak, LORD, for your servant is listening" (1 Samuel 3:10). When you read, adopt an attitude of listening. Try not to treat Scripture as a text, but as a personal message from God. What is he saying? What does it mean? What does it mean for my life? If you come to the Word focused on having an encounter with the Lord, he will speak to your heart, and you will be transformed.

An Important Note About the Responses to the Study Questions

Responses to the study questions are provided in the back of this Study Set. These responses do not exhaust the meaning that can be found in the Scripture reading. People will have unique insights. The responses have two important functions:

1. To provide participants with a review of each session, which will help establish a context for the reading and questions in the following session. The best time to read the responses is just before starting on the next session.
2. The second purpose of the responses is to provide guidelines for the small-group facilitators. **Facilitators:** Complete the Scripture reading and answer the questions on your own before reading the responses in preparation for facilitating the small-group discussion.

Participants should not review the responses for each session until after the session is completed. Although it might be tempting to look at these responses in advance, it is important to wait for the following reasons.

1. Bible study is not about simply watching a video presentation or reading a Bible commentary. It is just as important to immerse yourself in the Word of God itself and engage it with your heart and mind. The questions in *The Great Adventure* studies are designed to draw you into the Scriptures so that the Word of God will be planted and grow in your heart. Reading a response written by someone else may satisfy your mind for a moment, but it will not result in the kind of growth that will occur if you attempt to answer the question on your own first.

2. The success of a small group depends on a good discussion. A group of participants who have spent time pondering the Scripture passages on their own will have more varied insights to discuss.

For these reasons, please wait to read the responses until after the session. When you follow the steps of this study as intended, you will explore the Word of God in different ways—in the reading, the small-group discussion, the video presentation, and, finally, in the responses. Follow these steps over time and you will be more than fed—you will learn to feed yourself.

Ten Commandments of Small-Group Discussion

1. **Enjoy yourself!**
2. **Speak with respect and charity.**
3. **Do not ridicule or dismiss what others say. Keep comments positive.**
4. **Come prepared.**
5. **If you were not able to prepare, let others speak first.**
6. **Stick to the topic and questions at hand.**
7. **Start and end on time.**
8. **Allow silence. Give people a chance to think.**
9. **Listen to others without interrupting.**
10. **Keep personal matters within the group.**

Session 1 – Questions
Introduction to the Prophets

In many and various ways God spoke of old to our fathers by the prophets;
but in these last days he has spoken to us by a Son ...
– Hebrews 1:1-2

There are sixteen prophetic books in the Old Testament.[1] Taken as a whole, their length is equal to the entire New Testament. The importance of the prophetic books is incalculable, as it is nearly impossible to understand the work and message of Jesus without them.

Who were the prophets? What was their role in their own day? How should we read and understand their prophetic messages? These are some of the questions this study will answer.

As with other *Great Adventure* Bible studies, *The Prophets: Messengers of God's Mercy* strives to provide the "big picture"—the historical and theological context that prompted their messages—necessary to read and understand the prophets of the Old Testament. In ten sessions, we cannot study every prophet in depth, but we hope to stimulate your interest and lay out a clear road map for future study.

A key to understanding the prophets is to "read with the heart" and not just the mind. This is especially so for the prophetic books because they do not fall easily into any one particular literary genre. Some are anthologies or collections of oracles, narratives, and visions. All use poetic language, parallelism, hyperbole (i.e., exaggeration), symbols, and metaphors. At times, the prophets "act out" their messages. So we must be prepared to find meaning on multiple levels, particularly as we read about them in light of the person and work of Christ and the promise of his second coming.

What Is a Prophet?

The common Hebrew word for prophet is *nabi'*, which can mean one who is "called by the mouth" of God to "speak forth" his Word to the people of Israel.

There are different kinds of prophets represented in the Old Testament, but they all speak on behalf of God to his people in some way. God calls and equips each of them specifically for an individual task, and the prophets are often compelled to speak deeply unpopular messages.

A prophet speaks on behalf of God to his people.

If God's people had stayed close to him, there might have been no need for the prophets. They are sent at critical times to call the people back to their covenant relationship with God. Since the prophets speak to the "spiritually hard-of-hearing," they frequently have to shout or act in dramatic and startling ways. They proclaim the future consequences of continued sin, call people to repentance, and declare God's faithful love. They speak of the future in order to shed light on current events and to reveal God's plans and purposes.

[1] This number includes the book of Daniel, which is not listed among the prophets in the Old Testament; it is considered part of the "Writings."

Categories of Prophets: Former and Latter, Major and Minor

In the Hebrew Scriptures "the Prophets" *(Nevi'im)* refers not to a group of people but to the eight books that cover the time the people of God lived in the land of Israel, from their entry into Canaan through the Babylonian captivity.[2] Christian tradition classifies some of these books in the genre of history, but in the Jewish tradition, history itself has a prophetic character. The prophets of that time are not so much seers of the future as they are seers of the present—they look at what is happening around them in light of Israel's history with God; they discern lessons from that history; and they hear God's Word and convey it to the people. This history reminds the people of their covenant with God and the importance of keeping this covenant if they are to be blessed and remain in the Land of Promise. The telling of this history is therefore considered "prophetic."

You may have heard of the "former" and "latter" prophets, which is a way of dividing the prophets of the Hebrew canon. In this division, the term "former prophets" refers not to specific prophets but to the earlier books among the *Nevi'im.* They are easy to remember because these books are more historical in character. They are: Joshua, Judges, 1 and 2 Samuel, and 1 and 2 Kings. These books contain stories about prophets such as Elijah and Elisha, who do not have books named for them. The "latter prophets" are those classified in Christian tradition as the "prophets." Each book bears the name of a single prophet who is called by God to deliver a particular message. Therefore, these are also called the "writing prophets."

In this study, we will focus on the latter (or "writing") prophets. The latter prophets, in turn, are classified as "major" or "minor" prophets, based on the length of each one's prophetic book.

In Christian tradition, the **major prophets** are Isaiah, Jeremiah, Ezekiel, and Daniel. The books of the twelve **minor prophets** are shorter and may originally have been meant to be read as single books. These prophets are collectively known as "the Twelve" or "the Book of the Twelve."[3] In Jewish, Protestant, and Catholic Bibles, the minor prophets are placed after the major prophets and are arranged in the following order.[4]

Major Prophets	Minor Prophets ("The Twelve")
Isaiah	Hosea
Jeremiah	Joel
Ezekiel	Amos
Daniel	Obadiah
	Jonah
	Micah
	Nahum
	Habakkuk
	Zephaniah
	Haggai
	Zechariah
	Malachi

[2] These eight books are divided further in Christian Bibles. Samuel and Kings are two books each, and the final "Book of the Twelve" minor prophets is divided into twelve separate books.

[3] For example, Sirach 49:10 says, "May the bones of the twelve prophets revive from where they lie, for they comforted the people of Jacob and delivered them with confident hope."

[4] In the Hebrew canon, the book of Daniel is placed before Esther in the "Writings." Some Orthodox and Catholic Bibles follow a different arrangement of the minor prophets in accordance with the Septuagint.

The Biblical and Historical Context of the Prophets

We have already learned about the prophetic nature of the history of Israel. Knowing the broad outlines of that history will help us understand the message of the prophets and their place in the Bible.

At its heart, Israel's history—and, in fact, the entire narrative of the Bible—is a love story. It is the story of God reaching out to humanity and drawing us into a familial relationship with himself. After the relationship between God and man is broken in the Fall, God sets out to redeem mankind and restore them to his family through a series of covenants.

As Christians, we are members of the New Covenant in Jesus Christ. Before that, however, there was the Old Covenant (also called the Mosaic covenant), which was a binding agreement made by God with Israel and sealed with blood. By that covenant:

- God established the nation of Israel as his own people under his loving rule.
- God promised abundant blessings for those who kept its requirements.
- The people promised to keep God's Law or pay the price of breaking it.

The Mosaic covenant is later expanded when God establishes David as king and promises that he and his heirs will reign forever.

After the reigns of David and his son, Solomon, ten tribes split off from Judah, forming a kingdom based to the north of Jerusalem. The resulting "Northern Kingdom" keeps the name "Israel," while the "Southern Kingdom"—still ruled by the Davidic monarchy from Jerusalem—is thereafter called "Judah."

The Divided Kingdom At A Glance

	Northern Kingdom	**Southern Kingdom**
Name	Israel[5] ("Ephraim" or "Jacob")	Judah
Number of Tribes	Ten	Two
Ruler	Succession of kings, dynasties	Royal line of David
Center of Worship	Golden calves at Dan and Bethel	Temple at Jerusalem
Capital	Samaria	Jerusalem

Following this division, first Israel and then Judah—desiring to be like the nations around them—stray from God and begin to worship foreign gods. It is during the time of the Divided Kingdom that God begins to send the prophets. These "mouthpieces" (messengers of God) call Israel and Judah to return to their covenant relationship with God. In particular, the prophets do three things:

1. They call the people to **repentance**.
2. They warn of **judgment** that will follow as a consequence of not returning to the LORD and his covenant.
3. They point to a future **restoration** that will unite not just all of Israel but also, eventually, all the nations under the just reign of God and his anointed King (the Messiah).

5 "Israel" can refer to the Northern Kingdom or to the twelve tribes. The meaning must be inferred from the context.

The Great Adventure Bible Timeline Chart (included with this study) divides the biblical narrative into twelve distinct time periods to make it easy to get the "big picture" of salvation history before studying any part of the Bible. If you are not familiar with *The Bible Timeline* Chart, take a moment now to get your bearings.

The prophets we will study fall within three time periods of *The Bible Timeline:* the Divided Kingdom, the Exile, and the Return. As a memory aid, each section is color-coded: The black of the Divided Kingdom represents Israel's darkest period; the baby blue of the Exile evokes the people "singing the blues" in captivity; and yellow is used to signify the "brighter days" of the Return. Open the Chart so you can see these periods. Read the panel to the left of the black Divided Kingdom period, entitled, "Key to Understanding *The Bible Timeline* Chart."

In the colored band at the top of the Chart, you will find the **"narrative books"** of 1 and 2 Kings, Ezra, and Nehemiah. Together, these provide the basic historical context of the prophets. Toward the bottom of the Chart are other, **"supplemental" books** of the Bible that pertain to those periods.[6] Nearly all are the books of the writing prophets (for example, Obadiah, Joel, and Amos in the Divided Kingdom).

The colored band at the bottom of the Chart shows which nation is the **world power** at a particular time. This is crucial to know, as those nations have a strong influence on Israel and Judah both politically and spiritually. (See new *Bible Timeline* Chart.)

The center of the Chart shows the **progression of events** and the **key people** in the biblical narrative. It also has a **geographical aspect** to it. The center band represents the land of Canaan (Israel's home, the Promised Land). Events related to countries north of Israel (Assyria and Babylon, for example) are in the band above the center. Below are events related to countries to the south.

As for the people:

- Red names are people in **Jesus' genealogy line.**
- Names attached by lines to the bars in the middle of the Chart are the **kings** of the "Northern Kingdom" and "Southern Kingdom."
- Italicized names are **prophets.** Each is positioned near the kingdom or nation to which the individual prophet's message is directed (this will become clearer during the course of the study).

[6] The books called "supplemental" on *The Bible Timeline* Chart should not be considered less important than the fourteen "narrative books" that tell the story. They are placed on the Chart to show how they fit into the overall narrative.

The following chart lists the "writing" prophets of the Divided Kingdom, the Exile, and the Return, along with the primary audiences of their messages, the years they speak, and where you can read about them in the Bible. (Prophets included in this study are in bold.)

Writing Prophets of the Divided Kingdom, Exile, and Return

***Bible Timeline* Period**	**Audience and Context** (Israel exiled to Assyria, Judah to Babylon)	**Prophet**	**Years (BC)**	**Scripture Verses**
Divided Kingdom (North)	Israel (Pre-Exile)	Amos	760–753	Amos 2 Kings 14:23–15:7
		Hosea	750–715	Hosea 2 Kings 14:23–18:12
Divided Kingdom (South)	Judah (Pre-Exile)	**Isaiah**	740–680	Isaiah 2 Kings 15:1–20:21 2 Chronicles 26:16–32:33
		Micah	735–700	Micah 2 Kings 15:32–19:37 2 Chronicles 27:1–32:23
		Zephaniah	632–628	Zephaniah 2 Kings 22:1-2 2 Chronicles 34:1-7
	Judah (Pre-Exile, Exile)	**Jeremiah**	625–580	Jeremiah 2 Kings 22:3–25:30 2 Chronicles 34–36
	Judah (Pre-Exile)	Habakkuk	610–605	Habakkuk 2 Kings 23:31–24:7 2 Chronicles 36:1-8

Continued on next page

Continued from previous page

Bible Timeline **Period**	**Audience and Context** (Israel exiled to Assyria, Judah to Babylon)	**Prophet**	**Years (BC)**	**Scripture Verses**
Divided Kingdom (Other)	Edom			2 Kings 8:16-24 2 Chronicles 21:1-20
	Assyria	**Jonah**	800–753	Jonah 2 Kings 13:10-25, 14:23-29
Exile	Judah (Pre-Exile)	Joel	722–701	2 Kings 17–22 2 Chronicles 29-33
	Judah (Exile)	**Daniel**	605–535	Daniel 2 Kings 23:34–25:30 2 Chronicles 36:4-23
	Judah (Exile) Edom	**Ezekiel** Obadiah	590–571 c.586	Ezekiel, Obadiah 2 Kings 24:8-25, 30 2 Chronicles 36:9-21
	Assyria	Nahum	664–654	Nahum 2 Kings 21:1-18 2 Chronicles 33:1-20
Return	Judah (Post-Exile)	**Haggai**	520	Haggai Ezra 5:1–6:15
		Zechariah	520–480	Zechariah Ezra 5:1–6:15
		Malachi	432–424	Malachi Nehemiah 13:1-31

Maps

The Divided Kingdom

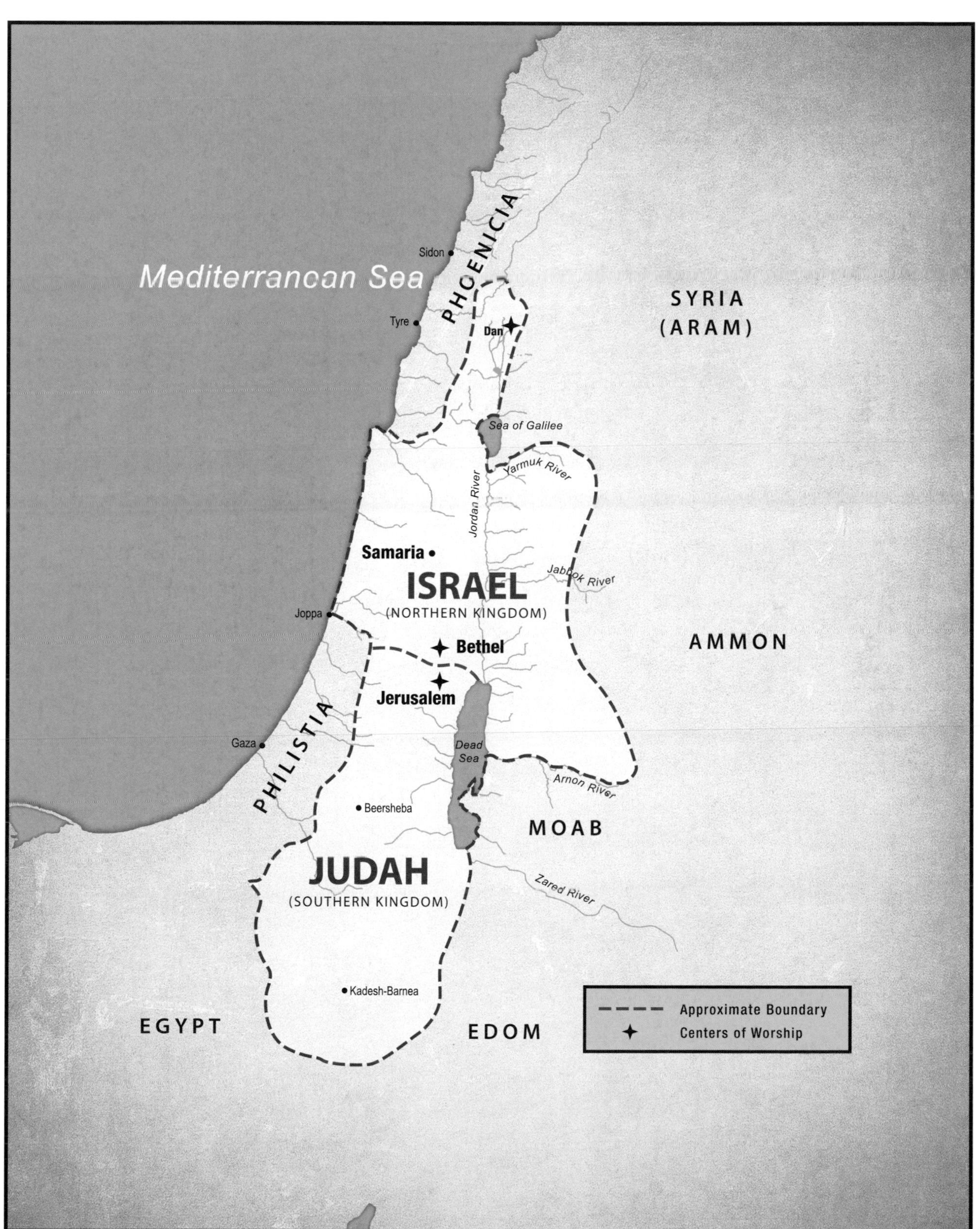

Assyrian Empire (c. 722 BC)

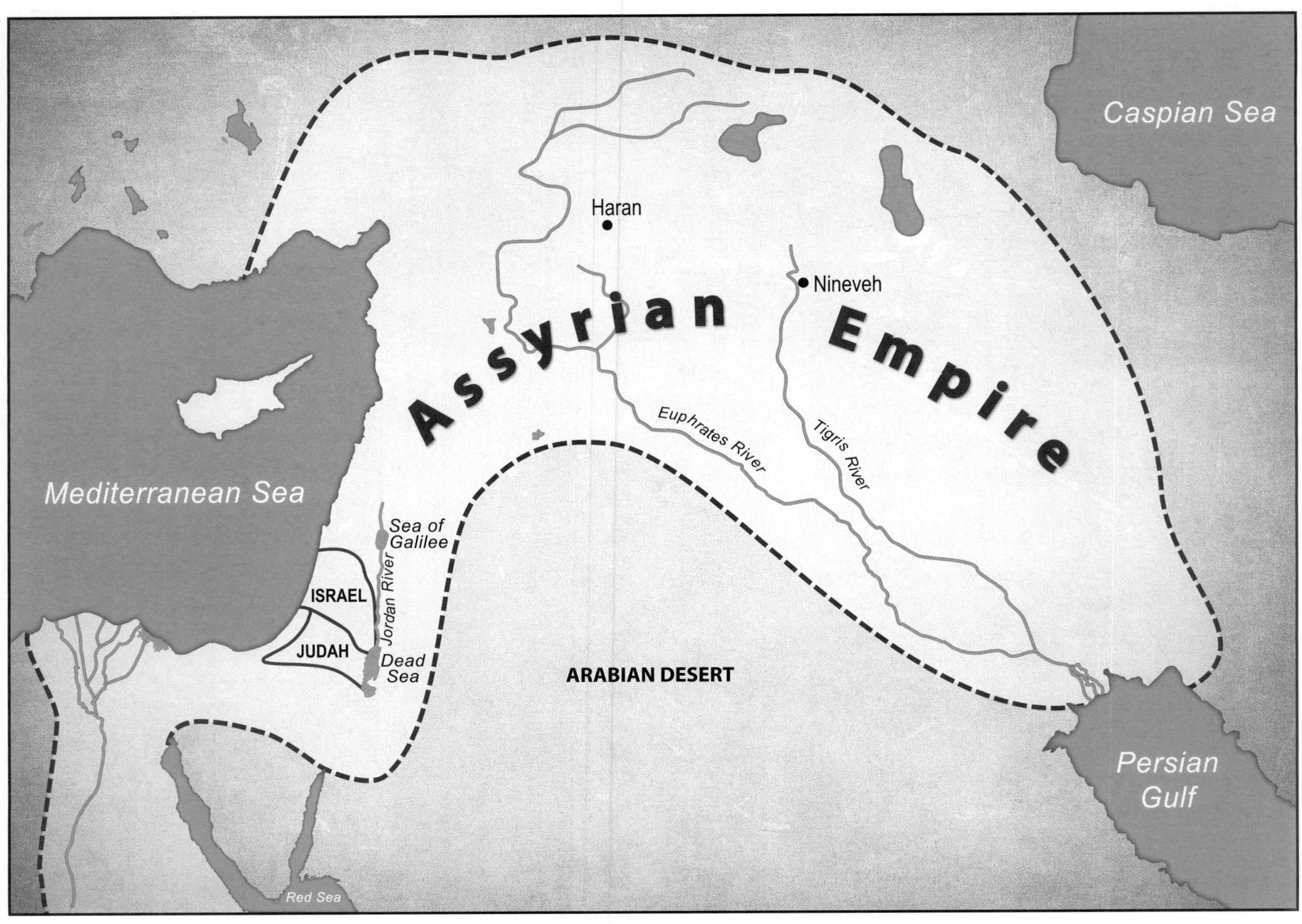

Babylonian Empire (c. 600 BC)

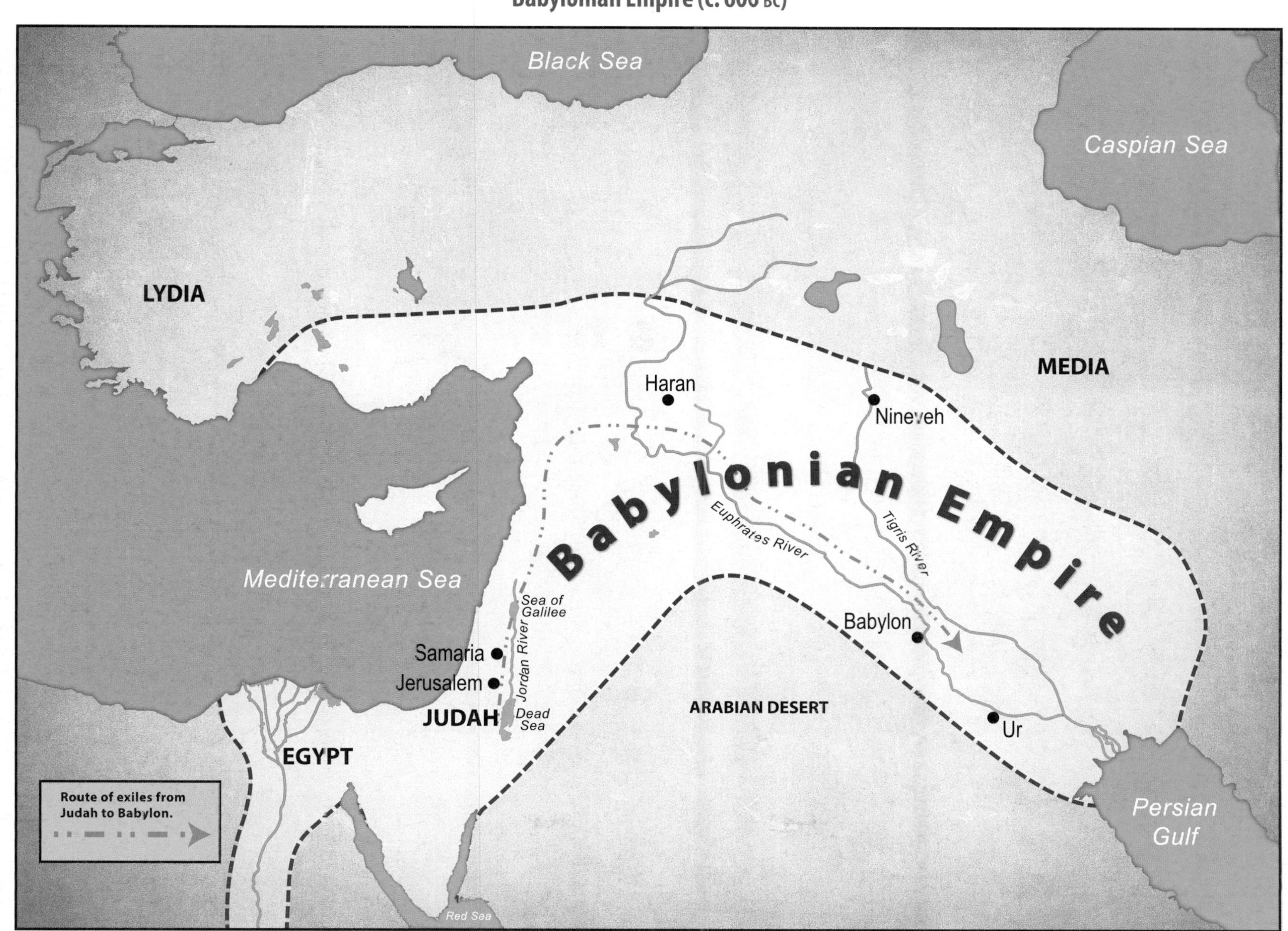

Persian Empire (c. 500 BC)

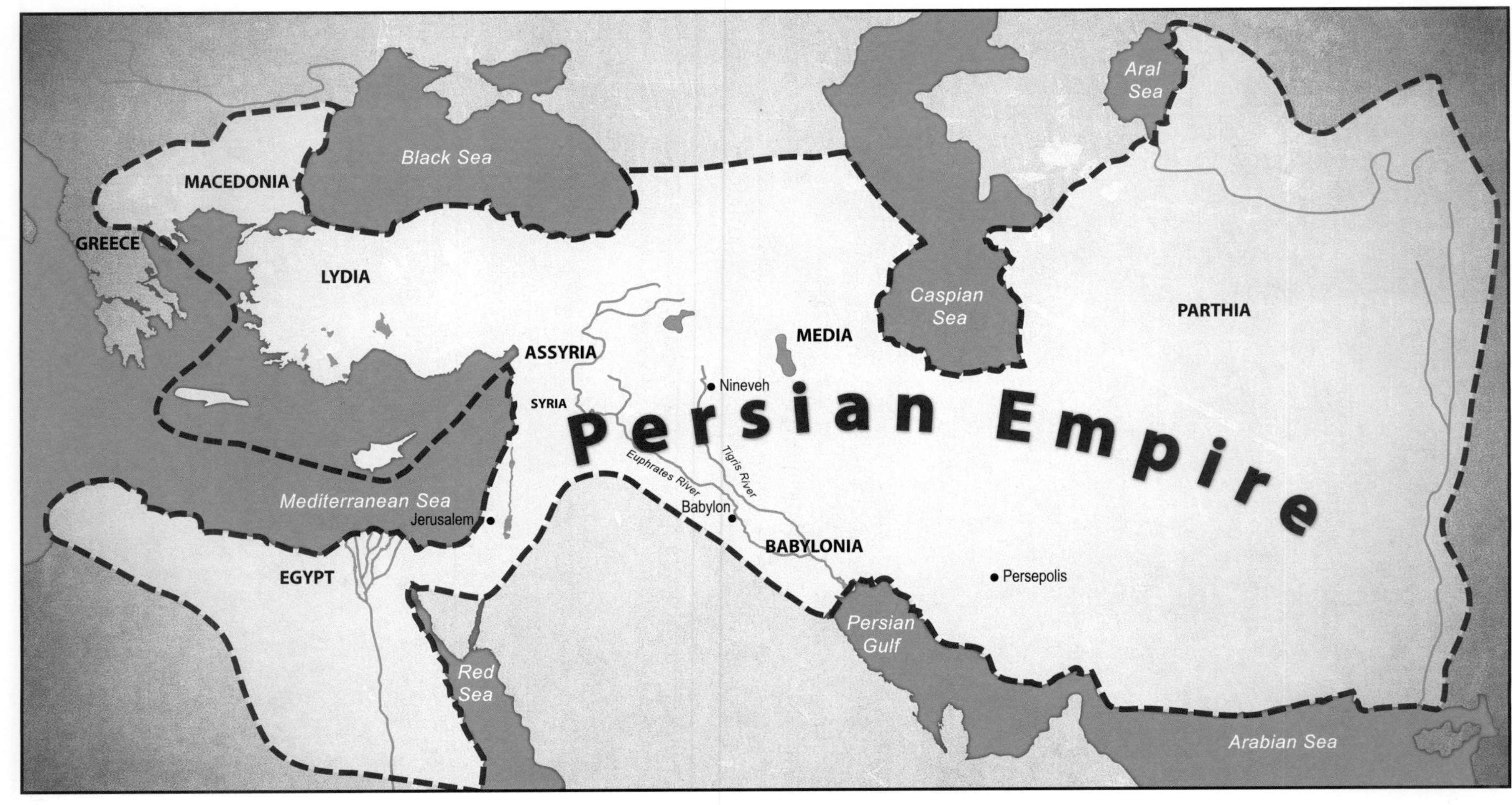

Messianic Prophecies from the Prophets and Their Fulfillment

Prophecy About the Messiah	Prophet	Fulfilled in Jesus
A prophet like Moses ("the Prophet")	Deuteronomy 18:15, 18	Acts 3:20-23 John 7:40-42
Born in Bethlehem	Micah 5:2	Matthew 2:1 Luke 2:4-6
Born of a virgin	Isaiah 7:14	Matthew 1:20-23 Luke 1:26-31
From King David's line, reign on his throne	Isaiah 9:7	Luke 1:32-33 Romans 1:3
Eternal throne	Daniel 2:44	Luke 1:33 Hebrews 1:8-12
Called Emmanuel	Isaiah 7:14	Matthew 1:23
Called out of Egypt	Hosea 11:1	Matthew 2:13-15
Way prepared by messenger	Isaiah 40:3-5; Malachi 3:1	Luke 3:3-6
Preceded by Elijah	Malachi 4:5-6	Matthew 11:13-14 Luke 1:17
Rejected by own people	Isaiah 53:1-3	Matthew 26:3-4 John 1:10-11, 7:5, 12:37-38
A sacrifice for sin	Isaiah 53:5-12	John 1:29 Acts 10:43, 13:38-39 Romans 5:6-8 1 Corinthians 15:3-4 Ephesians 1:7
Bring light to Zebulun and Naphtali, Galilee of the Gentiles	Isaiah 9:1-2	Matthew 4:13-16
How beautiful the feet of him who brings good news	Isaiah 52:7	Romans 10:15
Speak in parables	Isaiah 6:9 10	Matthew 13:10-15
Heal the brokenhearted	Isaiah 61:1-2	Luke 4:18-19
Carry our diseases	Isaiah 53:4	Matthew 8:17

Continued on next page

Continued from previous page

Prophecy About the Messiah	Prophet	Fulfilled in Jesus
God's Servant	Isaiah 42:1	Matthew 12:18
Called king, enter Jerusalem triumphantly on a donkey	Zechariah 9:9	Matthew 21:8-11 Mark 11:7-11 Luke 19:35-37 John 12:12-15
Betrayed for thirty pieces of silver	Zechariah 11:12-13	Matthew 26:14-16
Like a lamb to the slaughter	Isaiah 53:7	Acts 8:32
Tried and condemned	Isaiah 53:8	Matthew 27:1-2 Luke 23:1, 23 Acts 4:26-28
Silent before accusers	Isaiah 53:7	Matthew 27:12-14 Mark 15:3-5 1 Peter 2:22-23
Spat upon, struck	Isaiah 50:6	Matthew 26:67-68 Matthew 27:30 Mark 14:65, 15:19 John 19:1-3
Numbered with transgressors	Isaiah 53:12	Matthew 27:38 Mark 15:27-28 Luke 22:37, 23:32-33
Hands and feet pierced	Zechariah 12:10	John 20:25-27
Side pierced	Zechariah 12:10	John 19:34
Buried in a rich man's grave	Isaiah 53:9	Matthew 27:57-60
By his stripes we are healed	Isaiah 53:5	1 Peter 2:24
Every knee shall bow	Isaiah 45:23	Romans 14:11

Note: This prayer, Pope Francis' "Prayer of Renewal,"[7] will be prayed at the close of every session of this study.

Lord, I have let myself be deceived; in a thousand ways, I have shunned your love, yet here I am once more to renew my covenant with you. I need you. Save me once again, Lord, take me once more into your redeeming embrace.

[7] *Evangelii Gaudium* 3.

Session 1 Talk Notes

Introduction to the Prophets

I. Introduction

A. Definition: A prophet "afflicts the comfortable and comforts the afflicted" (Abraham Heschel)

B. Scope of this study

C. The "so what?" – relevance to us

1. The prophets' teachings are perennial, for everyone

2. The prophets are real people who share our struggles

3. The prophetic mission is our mission

4. The prophets reveal the Father's heart and point to Christ

a. Hugh of St. Victor quote from CCC 134

II. The "Who, What, When, Where, How, and Why" of the Prophets

A. What is a prophet?

1. What the prophets *do* reveals what a prophet *is*

2. "Prophet" from Greek *prophētēs,* equivalent to Hewbrew word *nabi* (to speak forth or to be called out)

3. A prophet: "one who is called out by the LORD to speak forth the Word of the LORD under the inspiration of the Holy Spirit"

B. Who were the Old Testament prophets?

1. Non-writing prophets (Genesis through 2 Kings) – Examples:

a. Abraham, an intercessor (Genesis 20:7)

b. Aaron, spokesperson for Moses (Exodus 7:1)

c. Nathan, a conscience for the king (2 Samuel 12)

d. Elijah and Elisha use predictive prophecy, signs, miracles to confront sin, call to repentance

2. Sixteen "writing prophets"

a. "Major" versus "minor" based on size of text

b. Major prophets (Christian tradition): Isaiah, Jeremiah, Ezekiel, Daniel

c. Minor prophets: Hosea through Malachi

i. Intended to be read together

ii. "The Book of the Twelve" (example: Sirach 49:10)

d. Eight covered in this study: Hosea, Jonah, Isaiah, Jeremiah, Ezekiel, Daniel, Haggai, and Malachi

C. When did the prophets speak, and to whom?

1. Three important time periods: Divided Kingdom, Exile, Return

2. Placement of prophets on *Bible Timeline* Chart indicates audience

3. See details in introduction to this study

4. Audiences: Northern and Southern Kingdoms, other nations

D. Where did the prophets come from?

1. Most prophesied in Judea, Jerusalem; others came from Galilee

2. All walks of life

E. What did the prophets say? (three central themes)

1. Call to repentance: healing a ruptured relationship

2. Judgment (consequences) for covenant infidelity

3. Hope, restoration, consolation

F. How did they relay this message?

1. Not "just the facts"

a. Use of images, metaphors, poetry, song

b. Aim to win hearts, not just heads

c. Prophets are living parables, embodying their messages

2. Hosea (next session) as an example

III. Conclusion: Pope Francis' Prayer of Renewal[8]

[8] For the text of this prayer, which is prayed at the close of each session, see page 12.

Prophets of the Divided Kingdom (930–722 BC)
Introduction to Sessions 2-6

The original kingdom of Israel was made up of twelve tribes ruled by a single king. This king was a descendant of King David, whose throne God had promised to establish forever in Jerusalem.

In 930 BC, the ten northern tribes revolted against the rule of David's grandson and split off from the two southern tribes, creating two separate kingdoms—Israel in the north and Judah in the south. (See the map on page 7.) Israel is often called "Ephraim" after the name of the largest northern tribe.

The first king of the Northern Kingdom, Jeroboam I, sets up two shrines with images of golden calves (one in Dan, in the northernmost part of the kingdom, and the other in Bethel, in the southernmost part). He also sets up a false priesthood and calendar of feasts to dissuade people from worshiping the one true God in the Temple in Jerusalem. Although Israel is first to turn away from God, Judah will soon turn its back on God's covenant as well. It is during the Divided Kingdom that God begins sending prophets to call his people back to himself.

Some prophets are sent to Israel (the Northern Kingdom). On your *Bible Timeline* Chart, locate the prophets in the period of the Divided Kingdom. These appear directly beneath the black "Northern Kingdom" bar. God sends Elijah and Elisha (two of the "former prophets") early in the period of the Divided Kingdom. When the situation becomes grave and exile is imminent, God sends the writing prophets **Amos** and **Hosea.**

God also sends prophets to other nations during this time. In the band above the center of the Chart, you will find **Jonah** (who is sent to Assyria) and **Obadiah** (who prophesies against Edom).

God calls other prophets to warn Judah (the Southern Kingdom), particularly around the time of the collapse of Israel in the north, that if they do not change their ways and turn back to the LORD, they will find themselves in a similar situation. The message to Judah is that it should not assume God's presence in the Temple will assure the people of divine protection. They must obey the covenant.

Find these prophets on the Chart where the first blue arrow shows Israel going into exile (above the purple "Southern Kingdom" bar). Notable among them are **Isaiah** and **Micah.** More prophets are sent to Judah closer to the time of that kingdom's defeat by Babylon. (Look for **Zephaniah, Jeremiah,** and **Habakkuk** on the Chart, just before Judah's downfall and the three deportations to Babylon, which are marked by three blue arrows).

The first four prophets we will study—**Hosea, Jonah, Isaiah,** and **Jeremiah**—are from the period of the Divided Kingdom.

A. Establish the Context

We begin our study with Hosea, the first of the twelve minor prophets.

The key to understanding this time in Israel's history and the message of the prophets in general is to recognize the nature of the covenant that was made between the LORD and Israel at Mount Sinai (Exodus 19–24). There, God promised to make the children of Israel his "own possession" (19:5) and "a kingdom of priests and a holy nation" (19:6). Israel, in turn, vowed to obey the LORD's commandments and be faithful to him. The resulting covenant formed a permanent bond of kinship; Israel has become God's family. In this context, a sin against God is an act of infidelity more than simply "breaking a law." God and his people are joined in a deep relationship in which God gives perfect love and faithfulness and expects love and faithfulness in return.

God calls Hosea to speak to the people of Israel (the ten northern tribes) toward the end of the reign of Jeroboam II in the middle of the eighth century BC. Under Jeroboam, the kingdom of Israel has prospered, but the people have strayed from God to worship the gods of Canaan. They have abandoned the very things that define them as a people of God—namely, worshiping him as the one true God; caring for the poor, widows, and orphans; and ruling with justice and righteousness. Instead, idolatry, injustice, and oppression are rampant. The people deserve the judgment that will follow their actions. Having turned from God to other sources of salvation, they will no longer benefit from his protection but instead will be thrown to the mercies of the nations they have sought.

As with many of the prophets, Hosea is called to do more than deliver God's message through words: He is called to live out that message in his life. In Hosea's case, God asks him to marry and remain faithful to a harlot to demonstrate God's loving faithfulness to unfaithful Israel. Hosea demonstrates to Israel and to us what it means to be in covenant relationship with the God who is just and all-powerful and who also *is* love.

Hosea's ministry lasts until the fall of Samaria in 722 BC, which marks the end of the Northern Kingdom. Before you begin your reading, take time to find the prophet and Jeroboam II on your *Bible Timeline* Chart. Although Hosea speaks in and to Israel, he is from Judah, and his message to Israel is meant to be a warning to the people of the Southern Kingdom as well. Thus, in the first verse, the book of Hosea names four kings of Judah—Uzziah, Jotham, Ahaz, and Hezekiah—along with Jeroboam II of Israel. Find their names on the Chart as well. They are in red, just below the purple "Southern Kingdom" bar.

The book of Hosea is the longest of the minor prophets, a beautiful book that reveals all of salvation history to be a love story between a faithful God and his beloved, yet unfaithful, people. It may be for this reason that Hosea is placed first among the Twelve, even though he is not the earliest of the minor prophets. Scholars have pointed out that the final prophetic book, Malachi, begins with, "'I have loved you,' says the LORD" (1:2) Thus, Hosea and Malachi, taken together, frame the others, providing a lens that helps us read the minor prophets and their messages of judgment and restoration in the context of God's loving plan.

Note: There are differences in verse numbering between the various English translations of Hosea. This study uses the Revised Standard Version–Catholic Edition (RSV-CE), which is the translation we recommend you use for this session.

B. Read the Story

Hosea can be divided into two unequal parts. Chapters 1–3 introduce Hosea, his mission, and God's message as it is lived out in Hosea's family. The remaining eleven chapters focus on the infidelity of the Northern Kingdom and God's covenant case against the people there, seen in light of his steadfast love. Read **Hosea 1:1–4:10 and Chapters 11 and 14** in one sitting to get a feel for the prophet's message and the metaphors he uses.

Going Deeper (optional): To get the entire story and message of Hosea, read the entire book.

As always, pray before you read.

C. Take a Deeper Look

Answering these questions will draw you into the heart of the story. If you do not understand something, make a note of it to bring up in the small-group discussion.

Hosea's Marriage and Children (Hosea 1–3)

1. The first chapter of Hosea gives us a snapshot of the entire book. Carefully re-read **Hosea 1:1–2:1.**

   a. If a prophet is one who speaks for God and reveals his heart, Hosea certainly does so in a unique and painful way. Explain how Hosea dramatically reveals God's heart to Israel.

   b. Hosea and Gomer have three children. Each name is a message, and as the years pass, the messages grow in seriousness. What is the meaning of each name? (Note: Some Bible versions provide only the English translations of the original Hebrew names. The list below is in order of appearance in the text.)

   Jezreel:[1]

   Lo-Ruhamah:

   Lo-Ammi:

---

1 Note: *Jezreel,* which means "scattered by God," is the name of the valley where Jehu slaughtered the royal family and usurped the throne of Israel prior to the time of Hosea. The king at the time of Hosea, Jeroboam II, is fourth of that line of kings.

c. Is there any hope that the judgments contained in these names might be reversed? (See **1:10–2:1** and **CCC 211.**)

2. Re-read **2:1-13,** where Hosea first states his case against Gomer (verses 1-7) and then unites it to God's charge against Israel in verses 8-13. What are some of Israel's chief sins? What does God say he will do about them?

3. Now read **2:14-23.**

   a. What is the ultimate motivation behind God's decision to withdraw his support from Israel?

   b. Describe the New Covenant God will make for them if they return.

Infidelity and Consequences (Hosea 4:1–14:1)

The rest of Hosea is composed of a number of oracles that are rich with poetic imagery. Like Chapter 2 of Hosea, this section begins with an indictment and ends with a plea for restoration.

4. Starting in Chapter 4, Hosea addresses the people of Israel directly. "The LORD has a controversy with the inhabitants of the land," he says in the first verse. This is legal terminology that implies a lawsuit over the broken Sinai covenant, in which Israel swore to follow only God and to keep his commands, which was a "marriage moment" between the LORD and his people.

   In 4:1, we read, "There is no faithfulness or kindness, and no knowledge of God in the land." According to verses 2-3, what are the consequences of the lack of these things in the lives of the people?

5. Hosea 4:6 says that Israel is "destroyed for lack of knowledge." The words "to know" and "knowledge of God" appear frequently in Hosea.[2]

   a. Consider the following verses, and record what you discover about the importance of "knowing" and "knowledge of God."

      Hosea 2:20: What is the basis of knowing God?

      Hosea 4:6: What is the result of "lack of knowledge" of God?

   b. **Think About It:** It is sobering to learn that roughly one-third of Catholics in the United States believe that God is merely an "impersonal force" rather than a personal Being with whom we can have a relationship.[3] What might that lack of the "knowledge of God" mean for attitudes and actions in our society? Do you see anything from Hosea's day reflected in our day?

6. In Hosea 2:19, God says he will betroth Israel to him "in steadfast love." The Hebrew word he uses, *hesed,* appears six times in Hosea, always in reference to the covenant faithfulness of the Lord. When Israel breaks that covenant, ending God's "legal" obligation to honor it, God's *hesed* reveals "its deeper aspect: It showed itself as what it was at the beginning, that is, as love that gives, love more powerful than betrayal, grace stronger than sin."[4]

   a. Read **Hosea 6:6.** What does God require of his people in return for his *hesed?*

   b. **New Testament Connection:** Jesus quotes Hosea 6:6 twice in the Gospel of Matthew. Read **Matthew 9:10-13.**[5] How does Jesus apply Hosea's words to his day?

---

[2] In Hebrew, the word *yadah,* "to know," means more than simply realizing or understanding something. It is based on experience or relationship and includes acting on knowledge. It can even refer to intimate sexual knowledge, as in Genesis 4:1, when Adam "knew" his wife. Similarly, "knowledge of God" *(da'at elohim)* means not just knowing *about* God but having a close and committed relationship with him, like a husband and wife.

[3] Pew Religious Forum on Religion & Public Life, "U.S. Religious Landscape Survey" (2008), as quoted in Sherry Weddell, *Forming Intentional Disciples: The Path to Knowing and Following Jesus* (Huntington, IN: Our Sunday Visitor, 2012), 43-44.

[4] St. John Paul II, *Dives in Misericordia* 4, note 52.

[5] Hosea 6:6 is also quoted in Matthew 12:7.

The Father's Love (Hosea 11)

7. Read **Hosea 11,** in which another metaphor is used to describe God's love for Israel. What is that metaphor? What does it teach us about God's heart and the motivation behind his actions?

8. ***Catechism* Connection:** We are not that different today than Israel was. Read **CCC 2787,** and comment on what the Church has to say about our relationship with God.

A Plea to Return (Hosea 14)

9. Hosea 12–13 details the many sins of Ephraim (Israel). The chapters end in loss and in the terrible judgment that will result from the people turning from God to foreign nations; but immediately after them comes a call to conversion. Read **Hosea 14:1-8,** and answer the following questions.

   a. In verses 1-3, what does Hosea call on Israel to do?

   b. What does God promise to do and be for the people in verses 4, 5, and 8?

   c. What advantages will these things have for Israel (verses 5-7)?

10. Imagine—God has plentiful grounds for "divorce," yet he asks to be reconciled. After all the people of Israel have done to him, how can he take them back? Read **CCC 218,** and comment on what you learn.

> The name "Hosea" is closely related in Hebrew to the name "Joshua" (in its Greek form, "Jesus"). It means—appropriately—"salvation." By making his life a living picture of God's love for Israel, Hosea illustrates in a way few others have, that God's essence is love. Hosea's life anticipates the life of Jesus: As Hosea purchases Gomer by his love and at his cost, so Jesus saves us from sin by his love and at the cost of his life.

D. Application

This question will help you apply one of the key themes of the session to your life. After meditating on it, respond to God with a brief written prayer if you choose.

Think back over what you have learned. In what sense are you *his* child and is God *your* Father? In what sense do you "know" God? In other words, what kind of relationship do you have with him? What part of Hosea's message speaks to you most—for yourself, for your family, or for those around you?

Dear Lord …

Session 2 Talk Notes

Hosea – Living God's Love Story

I. Setting the Stage

A. Background

B. Spiritual circumstances

C. Message also a warning to the South (Judah)

D. Hosea embodies his message in his life (response to marital infidelity)

1. Reveals the heart of God – like a literary Sacred Heart of Jesus
2. God's heart cry toward a rebellious child (Hosea 11:8)
   a. First Reading on feast of Sacred Heart
   b. "Ephraim" – Northern Kingdom
   c. My heart "recoils" (RSV-CE) = "is overwhelmed"; (NAB) – *nehpach:* to turn upside-down; "head over heels"
   d. A "literary crucifix"
3. Spousal language in Hosea 1–3

II. The Marriage Metaphor in Scripture

A. Genesis – marriage, one-flesh union

B. Exodus, a love story

1. Chapters 1–18: "God getting the girl"
2. Chapters 19–24: the "marriage ceremony" on Mount Sinai
   a. Ten Commandments = "ten wedding vows"
   b. Faithfulness to the covenant framed in marriage metaphor

C. Deuteronomy – the covenant fleshed out

D. Psalms – love language between Bridegroom and bride

E. Throughout the Prophets (example: Isaiah 54:5, "your Maker is your husband")

F. A way of seeing Luke and Acts (Bridegroom: Luke; bride: Acts)

G. Revelation – unveiling the Bridegroom (1–11) and the bride (12–22)

III. Hosea Embodies this Marriage Metaphor (Chapter 1)

A. God's terrible "to-do" – take a wife of harlotry (Hosea 1:2-3)

1. Gomer as a living symbol of Israel
2. Idolatry: spiritual infidelity (the "spirit of harlotry" – 4:12, 5:4)
3. "Knowing" as shared intimacy
4. What prostitution does to a marriage, idolatry does to relationship with God
5. Pope Francis: The opposite of faith is "idolatry"[6]

B. Hosea has a family with Gomer (Chapter 1)

1. Names of children symbolize Israel's spiritual situation
    a. *Jezreel* – "to be scattered by God"
    b. "Not pitied" *(Lo-Ruhamah)* – literally, "without a womb"; love-less
    c. "Not my people" *(Lo-Ammi)*
    d. Message: If you do not repent, you will be these things
2. "Gomer" means "It's over"

C. God proposes a reversal if they return to him (Chapter 2)

1. Hosea's and God's hearts blend together
2. "Plead with your mother" (2:2) – a summons to divorce court
3. Gomer takes the stand – "I will go after my lovers" (RSV-CE: 2:5; NAB: 2:7)
4. Hosea tries to get Gomer back ("tough love")
5. Gomer, like Israel, persists

D. God's faithfulness to their infidelity, lived out by Hosea (Chapter 3)

1. Hosea buys Gomer back, imaging God's love
2. The price paid shows his desperation
3. Hosea redeems Gomer; a symbol of Christ our Redeemer
4. Verse 3: You shall not live this life anymore

IV. The Rest of Hosea: Unpacking the Covenant Lawsuit

A. Three charges (Chapter 4): no faithfulness *(emet),* kindness *(chesed),* or knowledge *(da'ath)* of God in the land

B. At end, a word of hope (Chapter 14): I will heal you of your faithlessness; return to me

V. Conclusion: Prayer of Renewal[7]

6 *Lumen Fidei* 13.

7 For the text of this prayer, which is prayed at the close of each session, see page 12.

A. Establish the Context

As we saw in the previous session, the Book of the Twelve begins with Hosea's dramatic demonstration of God's love for his wayward people. The next three minor prophets—Joel, Amos, and Obadiah (who we will not study in this program)—deplore the sins of Israel and the nations and pronounce judgment while announcing the future restoration of God's kingdom. They say nothing of including the nations in that restoration, however, and the book of Jonah follows them with a qualifying message. **As Hosea was all about love, Jonah is all about mercy:** God's compassion and willingness to forgive all who turn to him, both Jew and Gentile. As Jonah learns, God is Lord of all creation and all nations. Even Assyria—the epitome of wickedness and the recipient of his message—can be delivered if it repents.

Who Is Jonah?

The prophet is identified in 1:1 as "Jonah the son of Amittai"—a prophet of the Northern Kingdom named in 2 Kings 14:25-27, who prophesied during the reign of Jeroboam II, predicting that the king would restore the northern borders of Israel. It is worth getting the larger context from 2 Kings. Jeroboam did what was "evil in the sight of the Lord" (2 Kings 14:24), but the Lord nonetheless gave him military success. Jonah would have witnessed an outpouring of blessing on Israel at a time when the people persisted in their sins and were very far from God (see 2 Kings 17). This is the prophet God calls, then, to take a message of mercy to Nineveh in Assyria, which had launched a ruthless empire-building campaign by the end of Jeroboam's reign. It is to Assyria that Israel will fall in 722 BC, never to recover. This forms the background to the book of Jonah.

When Was the Book Written?

The author of the book of Jonah and the date of its composition are unknown. Based on the language used and its message, many scholars believe it was written post-exile, in the mid-fifth century BC. Its message would speak loudly to the Jews of that era, centuries after the fall of Israel and during the return of Judah from Babylonian exile. Many Jews at that time thought God loved only Israel and hated its pagan neighbors. For them, reading about Jonah's mission to Nineveh with the benefit of hindsight, Assyria meant wickedness as certainly as the Third Reich does to modern Jews. The message of God's mercy on such a place and people would be profound. At that time, Israel (the Northern Kingdom) remained in exile. But Judah, which, like Jonah, fled from God's presence, was given a second chance and restored to the land. What, then, was their relationship to the nations? The question at the end of the book of Jonah is for them as well.

Is the Story of Jonah True?

The study of Jonah often starts with the question, "Did it really happen?" The majority of modern scholars consider Jonah to be a parable or allegory, but the Church does not require us to believe one way or the other.

Could the story of Jonah have happened as described? Of course. The omnipotent God who raised Jesus from the grave and calmed the seas is perfectly able of commanding a "great fish" to swallow a man and spit him out, alive and kicking, three days later (see Jonah 1:17). *Did* it happen? This is harder to say. The book is presented as an historical narrative, but some of its literary features suggest something more like a fable (e.g., it has humorous elements, lacks historically identifiable facts, makes use of larger-than-life caricatures of people and things, and is full of literary motifs). For example, Nineveh is a symbol for wickedness akin to Sodom and Gomorrah in Genesis and the "ends of the earth" (i.e., Tarshish). Even Jonah's name, which means "dove," is rich in symbolism; it represents Israel itself, atoning sacrifice, and a sign from God. Regardless of whether the story actually happened as told, the book of Jonah is certainly "true" in what it teaches. In our look at this prophet, we will set the question of historicity aside and focus on the message that God and the inspired author of this book of the Bible intended to convey to God's people then and today.[1]

B. Read the Story

Read the entire book of **Jonah** in one sitting to get a feel for the prophet's message (it is only four short chapters).

As always, pray before you read.

C. Take a Deeper Look

Answering these questions will draw you into the heart of the story. If you do not understand something, make a note of it to bring up in the small-group discussion.

The Reluctant Prophet (Jonah 1)

1. When the Word of the LORD comes to the prophet Jonah, telling him to cry out against the "great city" of Nineveh because of its wickedness, Jonah's response is to flee on a ship to Tarshish.

    a. Find Joppa, Jonah's starting point, on the map on this page. Locate Nineveh, where he is asked to go, and Tarshish, where he decides to go instead. What do you notice?

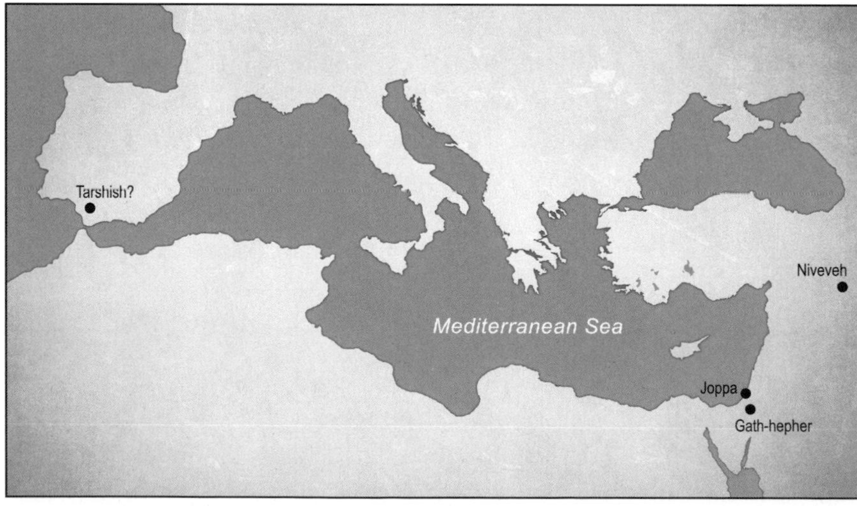

    b. Jonah's reluctance to go to Nineveh is understandable in light of Assyria's fearsome, tyrannical rule. Yet, it is not Nineveh he seems to be afraid of. From what does Jonah flee, according to verses 2, 3, and 10?

[1] For more on the literal and spiritual senses of Scripture, see CCC 115–119.

c. Read **Genesis 3:8 and 4:16.** Who else have we seen flee in this way? How were their circumstances similar to or different from Jonah's?

2. Compare and contrast Jonah's response to God's Word to the response of the captain, the mariners, the fish, the wind, and the sea. Note the verses where you find your answers.

3. Describe the progressive downward spiral that parallels Jonah's trip "away from the presence of the Lord" in **1:3, 1:5, 1:15, 1:17, 2:5, and 2:6a** (NAB: 1:3, 1:5, 1:15, 2:1, 2:6, and 2:7a).

4. Read **Psalm 139:1-12.**

   a. How is the truth of this psalm reflected in Jonah 1?

   b. How have you experienced the far-reaching persistence of God's love?

How Long Was Jonah in the Whale's Belly?

"Three days and three nights" (1:17) was a conventional phrase in Hebrew for "parts of three days" that could mean anywhere from twenty-six to seventy-two hours. Centuries later, Jesus would compare his own "three days and three nights in the heart of the earth" (Matthew 12:40) with Jonah's time in the belly of the whale. That time, as we know, was not a full seventy-two hours but lasted from late Friday afternoon to early Sunday morning.[2]

---

[2] While we measure days beginning at dawn (technically, at midnight), the Hebrews counted days from sunset, following Genesis 1:5, NAB: "Evening came, and morning followed—the first day."

God Gets Jonah's Attention (Jonah 2)

In Chapter 1, the Word of the LORD came to Jonah, and Jonah ran away. In Chapter 3, the Word of the LORD will come to Jonah a second time, and this time, he will obey. What happens between the two episodes is "a whale of a story"—Jonah spends three days and nights in the belly of a "great fish," according to the narrative. Whether one reads this as historical fact or as parable, Chapter 2 holds the key to understanding the change in Jonah.

5. Read **Jonah 2.** In verse 1 (NAB: verse 2), we read that Jonah prays from the belly of the fish. How does Jonah describe the place from which he cries to God in verses 1-6 (NAB: verses 2-7)?

6. Describe Jonah's prayer in 2:1-9 (NAB: 2:2-10) as it reflects his change of heart.

7. Recall the many times Jonah has "gone down" lower and lower, away from the LORD (see your response to question 3). What is God's response to Jonah's distress? See **verse 6** (NAB: verse 7).

God Calls Jonah Again (Jonah 3)

The Word of God comes to Jonah again, and this time, he obeys and goes to Nineveh. The description of the city as "three days' journey in breadth" (3:3) has caused some to doubt the historicity of this account, because there is no record of Nineveh approaching such a great size. Some possible interpretations: Three days may have been the expected length of Jonah's task, the size of the entire region around Nineveh, or a deliberate mirroring of Jonah's three days in the fish's belly.

8. Read **Jonah 3.** Given the reputation of the people of Nineveh, one might expect their reaction to Jonah's message to be similar to the reaction Lot's sons-in-law had to God's message that the city of Sodom would be destroyed (see **Genesis 19**): Lot's family thought he was joking and had to be forcibly removed to be saved.

   a. Describe the response of the people of Nineveh to Jonah.

b. Describe the response of the king and his motivation in verses 6-10. How would you compare him with the captain in 1:6? What does each know about God?

9. How is the prophecy from **Jeremiah 18:7-8** borne out in God's response to Nineveh's repentance?

10. **New Testament Connection:** Read **Matthew 12:38-42.** What meaning does Jesus give Jonah's story in applying it to his generation?

God Gets Jonah's Attention Again (Jonah 4)

11. **Think About It:** When Jonah says, "I knew that thou art a gracious God and merciful, slow to anger, and abounding in steadfast love" (4:2), he is quoting God's own words in Exodus 34:6-7. In that passage, God declared his mercy in the context of Israel turning from him to the Golden Calf even as he was establishing his covenant with them. In spite of their wickedness, God forgave them and took them as his own. Knowing this about God, why is Jonah angry? How can he use these words to justify his flight to Tarshish?

12. a. Jonah would rather die than carry God's message of mercy to Nineveh. Now, in Chapter 4, he asks to die rather than witness this mercy. Explain how God gets Jonah's attention in verses 6-9.

b. What message does God intend Jonah to learn from this? (See **verses 10-11.**)

D. Application

This question will help you apply one of the key themes of the session to your life. After meditating on it, respond to God with a brief written prayer if you choose.

Have you ever run (or are you running now) from God? Or is there someone you think does not deserve mercy? Who is it? What prevents you from bearing God's message to them or showing them mercy? With this in mind, what lesson or lessons can you take from Jonah and apply in that situation?

Dear Lord …

Session 3 Talk Notes

Jonah – God's Reluctant Messenger

I. Setting the Stage

A. Background

B. A reflection on the merciful character of God

C. Audience and their response

D. Jonah's reluctance: a liturgical contrast

1. Response of faith or fear (feasts of Jonah and St. Matthew, September 21)
2. Two runaways (Jonah paired with Prodigal Son, Twenty-Seventh Week in Ordinary Time)

E. Masterful storytelling

F. Jewish oral tradition: Jonah as a disciple of Elisha[3]

II. Jonah and the Great Fish (Chapter 1)

A. God calls Jonah and Jonah flees

1. Why? Jonah knows the heart of God
2. The distance of Tarshish – "from afar" (Isaiah 60:9)
3. The irony of trying to escape the LORD's presence
    a. God will never leave or forsake you (Deuteronomy 31:6; Hebrews 13:5; Matthew 28:20)
    b. God's persistent, pursuing love
        i. Francis Thompson, "The Hound of Heaven"
        ii. St. Augustine: "Our hearts are restless till they find rest in thee"

B. The storm

1. Pagan sailors ask Jonah to call on God for mercy
2. Irony: fleeing from God on the sea God made
3. Sin, however private, affects others
4. Sailors' response
    a. Risk lives to save Jonah
    b. Ask God's forgiveness before throwing Jonah overboard
    c. Offer sacrifices, make vows

---

3 See Louis Ginzberg, *The Legends of the Jews,* XIII, p. 246ff.

C. Jonah in the belly of the fish

1. Truth or parable?

2. Judgment or mercy?
   a. "Appointed," *suwm* = "extended compassion"

III. Jonah's Deliverance (Chapter 2)

A. Thanksgiving *(todah)* psalm

1. Move from plight, to acknowledging God and declaring deliverance, to thanks

2. Jonah's flight takes him down, yet straight to God

3. Psalm ends with thanksgiving, promises to sacrifice, vows

B. The obedience of the fish (2:10)

IV. Jonah Called Again (Chapter 3)

A. The God of second chances

B. Jonah obeys, but not from the heart

C. The message (verse 4): "Yet forty days, and Nineveh shall be overthrown!"

1. Nineveh calls for a fast

2. Ashes at start of a forty-day call for repentance: Lent

V. Jonah's Continued Reluctance (Chapter 4)

A. God works with Jonah

B. An open question at the end

C. **New Testament Connection:**

1. **Acts 1:8 – structure of Acts**

2. God intends gospel to go to all nations

3. Acts 10: Peter ("Simon Bar-Jona")[4] says "yes" in Joppa

4. Will you be a Jonah or a Peter?

VI. Conclusion: Prayer of Renewal[5]

---

[4] Peter is called Simon Bar-Jona ("Simon, Son of Jonah") in Matthew 16:17.

[5] For the text of this prayer, which is prayed at the close of each session, see page 12.

A. Establish the Context

In this session, we move from the minor prophets to Isaiah, the first—and perhaps the greatest—of the major prophets. The opening verses of Isaiah place him firmly in the same time period as Hosea by naming the same four kings of Judah: Uzziah, Jotham, Ahaz, and Hezekiah. The main "villain" we encounter in Isaiah has been introduced to us in Jonah: Assyria, whose capital is Nineveh.

Hosea, you may recall, speaks to Israel, the Northern Kingdom. He expresses God's heart-cry to the people, who have abandoned him to worship other gods, and he warns that the consequence of continued infidelity will be exile. The northern kings do not listen to Hosea. Instead of returning to the Lord, they scramble to build foreign alliances—particularly as Tiglath-pileser comes to power in Assyria and begins a series of aggressive, empire-building campaigns that threaten Israel's existence.

In this session, we will see how the struggles in Israel affect Judah. King Pekah of Israel threatens to invade Judah, which is ruled by King Ahaz, if Ahaz will not join his anti-Assyrian alliance. Isaiah is called upon to advise Ahaz, and he warns him that Israel will be conquered as the consequence of its persistent unfaithfulness and reliance on other nations rather than on God. This prediction comes true in 722 BC. When Israel is conquered, Judah is spared, but the reprieve is short-lived. In 701 BC, Assyria's king, Sennacherib, takes a huge army to the gates of Jerusalem and threatens Judah as well.

The first half of the book of Isaiah is set during this crucial time period. Like Hosea, Isaiah gives voice to God's strong and loving cry to his children. This voice is full of warning and promises of judgment in Chapters 1–39, which, taken together, have been called the "Book of Woe." While the people of Judah watch the fall of Israel from the sidelines, they should not think they are immune to the consequences of turning from God simply because they possess Jerusalem, the Temple, and a Davidic king. God calls Judah to repent and gives the people multiple signs of his will to save them for the sake of his promise to King David.

For now, we will focus on the first thirty-nine chapters of the book of Isaiah, leaving the second half of the book—the "Book of Consolation"—for the next session. Given Isaiah's scope and richness, our aim in both sessions is simply to present an overall picture of the whole.

Regarding authorship: It is not known for certain whether Isaiah wrote the entire book or whether Chapters 40–55 and 56–66 were written by one or more others (called "Second Isaiah" and "Third Isaiah"). Most scholars agree that the book holds together as a literary and theological unit. For the purposes of this study, we will refer to the author of all sixty-six chapters as Isaiah.

And now, the "Book of Woe" …

B. Read the Story

We recommend that you read **Isaiah 1–12 and 36–39** in one sitting. As with many of the prophetic books, Isaiah is not a seamless narrative but a collection of oracles. Do not worry about understanding everything; simply read to get a feel for what is written. The following questions will help you take a deeper look at some of the highlights.

Going Deeper (optional): To get the entire story and message of Isaiah's "Book of Woe," read **Isaiah 1–39.** Further background can be found in **2 Kings 16–20.**

As always, pray before you read.

C. Take a Deeper Look

Answering these questions will draw you into the heart of the story. If you do not understand something, make a note of it to bring up in the small-group discussion.

God Reasons with Israel and Calls for Repentance (Isaiah 1)

Isaiah 1:1 introduces the author, his audience, and the overall historical context. If you have not done so yet, find the kings named there on your Bible Timeline *Chart.*

1. In 1:2-4, "The LORD" (literally, "YHWH," the God who established a covenant with his people) lays out his case against Judah.

   a. What are the charges?

   b. Compare these charges to the charges God levels against Israel in **Hosea 4:1-6.** How are they similar? Why is this significant? (See questions 4-6 in Session 2.)

2. The sacrifices Hosea condemns in Israel are made at false altars to false gods (see **Hosea 2:13 and 8:13**). In Isaiah 1, God rejects Judah's sacrifices made to him in the Temple in Jerusalem. Why? (See **Isaiah 1:12-15,** and read **CCC 2100** for insight into this question.)

3. God lays two paths before his people in Isaiah 1:18-20. What are the two paths, and where do they lead? (See also **verse 27.**)

4. **Think About It:** What does the first chapter of Isaiah reveal about God's heart and desire?

The Call of Isaiah (Isaiah 6)

In Isaiah 5, God sings a plaintive love song for his beloved Judah, which is overrun with injustice like an abandoned vineyard with thorns. He pronounces a series of woes on the land; as a consequence of Judah's rebellion, judgment is at hand. God will "whistle for" (5:26) a foreign nation to invade them and carry them off into exile. It is against this backdrop that Isaiah in Chapter 6 tells of his call, which comes at a crucial time. "The year that King Uzziah died" (6:1) marks the end of a time of peace and prosperity and the start of Tiglath-pileser of Assyria's ruthless, empire-building crusades. God will allow this looming threat to overcome his people if they do not return to his loving care.

5. Read **Isaiah 6:1-8.**

   a. Consider the details of Isaiah's vision. What do they tell you about God?

   b. **New Testament Connection:** Centuries later, the apostle John is given a similar vision in Revelation 4:1-8. What similarities do you see between the two descriptions?

   c. Think about what the angels say in this passage. Does it sound familiar? At what part of the Mass do we enter into this angelic praise of God's holiness? What do we say?

6. Read all of **Isaiah 6.**

   a. Based on this chapter, what kind of a man is Isaiah?

   b. **Think About It:** What might be discouraging or encouraging about the details of Isaiah's calling? Is there encouragement in the fact that he himself is cleansed?

7. ***Catechism* Connection:** Read **CCC 208,** and consider what you have read in Isaiah 6. What ramification does the holiness of God have for people who are separated from him by sin?

"The Lord Himself Will Give You a Sign" (Isaiah 7:14)

That Isaiah's lips are cleansed is a sign of what God is willing to do for all his people if they will return to him. This "call story" prepares us for two signs of hope that God will send to two very different kings: Ahaz and his son, Hezekiah. Consult your Bible Timeline *Chart if you need a reminder of their place in the "big picture."*

8. By the days of King Ahaz, Judah is in crisis. Israel (Ephraim)[1] and Syria have joined against Assyria, and they are attempting to force Judah to join their revolt. As an alternative, Ahaz enters into a protection treaty with Assyria, requiring Judah vassals to pay tribute to and worship Assyrian gods.[2] Isaiah is a court prophet with Ahaz's ear, and he speaks to him for the Lord. Read **Isaiah 7:1-9.** What message does he bring?

9. This message bears with it the hope that Ahaz will put his trust in God and not in political alliances. Isaiah asks Ahaz to request a sign—which he refuses to do. But God himself gives Ahaz a sign for the house of David. Read **Isaiah 7:10-17.**

   a. The sign is a familiar one. Describe it and the One who is promised.

God Gives Ahaz a Sign

Efforts to explain the sign of Emmanuel within its immediate historical context have largely failed. "The passage about the virgin who gives birth to Emmanuel," Pope Benedict XVI wrote, "is a word in waiting."[3] That Word, Christians believe, came to pass when a virgin of Nazareth gave birth to one who is truly "Emmanuel," God with us. Pope Benedict continues: "Marius Reiser has summed up the way Christian readers have experienced this passage as follows: 'The prophet's prediction is like a miraculously formed keyhole, into which the key of Christ fits perfectly'" (Bibelkritik, 328).[4]

1 "Ephraim," the name of the largest tribe in the north, was sometimes used to refer to the entire Northern Kingdom, Israel. "The house of David" in verse 2, refers to the kingdom of Judah.

2 See 2 Kings 16:7, 10-18.

3 Pope Benedict XVI (Joseph Ratzinger). *Jesus of Nazareth: The Infancy Narratives* (New York: Random House, 2012), 50-51.

4 Ibid.

b. The sign of a coming child echoes through the next few chapters. Read **Isaiah 9:6-7** (NAB: 9:5-6). What role and characteristics will he have?

10. In Isaiah 11:1, the expected Savior-child is described as "a shoot from the stump of Jesse" (i.e., a King from the royal line of Jesse's son David, which will have been cut off by that time).

    a. Read **11:2-5,** and list the characteristics of this future anointed King.

    b. Read **11:10-12, 16.**[5] What will this "root of Jesse" accomplish?

Hezekiah's Victory (Isaiah 36–39)

In 722 BC, toward the end of Ahaz's reign in Judah, the prediction that came with the sign in Isaiah 7 comes to pass as Assyria sweeps into the Northern Kingdom of Israel, conquering Samaria and resettling most of the population in other parts of the Assyrian Empire. Israel is no more.

In 715 BC, Ahaz's son, Hezekiah, succeeds him to the throne. The situation in Judah becomes dire, with no buffer between it and the continued onslaught of Assyria. We have already seen that the people of Judah rely on religious ritualism while their hearts are far from God. Politically, there is constant pressure to turn to other nations—instead of to God—for help.

11. In 701 BC, Sennacherib brings his huge Assyrian army to the gates of Jerusalem and the "Rabshakeh" (called the "the commander" in the NAB) delivers a message.

    a. Read **Isaiah 36:13-20.** What challenge does Isaiah bring to the people?

    b. Now read Hezekiah's response to this challenge in **37:1-4 and 37:14-20** (where he responds when it comes a second time). Explain how Hezekiah lives up to his name, which means, "God is my strength."

[5] Note: In Isaiah 11:10, "stand as an ensign" ("set up as a signal" in the NAB) means to put up a banner or raise a flag for the nations to gather around.

c. Read **37:33-38.** What is the result? What does this say about God?

D. Application

This question will help you apply one of the key themes of the session to your life. After meditating on it, respond to God with a brief written prayer if you choose.

Do you wonder where Hezekiah finds the strength of faith he needs to face Sennacherib? Isaiah 38 gives us a clue. A year prior to the Assyrian invasion, Hezekiah's fervent prayers on his deathbed had brought him personal healing and a reprieve for the nation: fifteen additional years of life and a promise that God would deliver him and Jerusalem from Assyria. His beautiful prayer of thanksgiving and devotion to the LORD is recorded there as well. Spend some time reading this chapter and meditating on it. Has there been a time in your life when God has intervened on your behalf? Can this strengthen you for future battles?

Dear Lord …

Session 4 Talk Notes

Isaiah Part 1 – Prophet of Woe

I. Setting the Stage

A. Background and scope

B. Two-part division

1. "Book of Woe" (Chapters 1–39) – "Afflict the comfortable"
2. "Book of Consolation" (Chapters 40–66) – "Comfort the afflicted"

C. A call to covenant faithfulness

II. Isaiah 1 as an "Overture" – Key Themes Introduced (Chapter 1)

A. The problem (verses 2-4)

1. Covenant infidelity (language of father-child)
2. They do not know the Lord

B. God revealed as the Holy One of Israel, *Kadosh Israel* (verse 4)

1. A title nearly exclusive to Isaiah
2. Repetition provides inner unity to Isaiah
3. The Holy One issues an appeal to holiness (verse 18)
   a. "Come now, let us reason together" – I can make you clean
   b. Importance of cooperation
   c. CCC 1470 on the sacrament of reconciliation

III. God Lays Out His Case Regarding Covenant Infidelity (Chapters 1–5)

A. Summation of charges (1:21-23)

1. The "faithful city" (Jerusalem) "has become a harlot"
2. Violence, treachery, lack of love for the poor

B. Expanded in chapters to come

IV. God Calls Isaiah (Chapter 6)

A. Vision of God enthroned

B. Song of the Seraphim

1. *Kadosh, kadosh, kadosh* – holy to the highest degree
2. Parallel in book of Revelation

C. Isaiah's response ("Woe is me")

1. He confesses his sin
2. "Woe" used eight times in Isaiah 3–5 to describe Judah

3. Isaiah identifies with his people

D. Isaiah purified, set apart (verses 6-7)

1. Burning coal to unclean lips before he speaks for God
2. Liturgical connection to Eucharist: Mass of St. John Chrysostom
3. St. John of Damascus: "Let us take hold of the divine coal [the Eucharist], so that the fire of our longing, fed by the flame of the coal, may purge away our sins"[6]

E. Isaiah's mission and response: "Here am I! Send me" (verse 8)

1. The people resist

V. Historical Account of King Ahaz (Chapters 7–8)

A. Syria and Israel try to force Ahaz (Judah) to join them against Assyria

B. Ahaz's choice: fear or faith?

C. The Lord gives Ahaz a sign

1. A virgin will conceive and bear a Son, Immanuel (7:14)
2. Who is the Son? The prophecy is:
   a. "A word in waiting" (Pope Benedict)[7]
   b. "A miraculously formed keyhole into which the key of Christ fits perfectly"[8]

D. The multiple layers of prophetic fulfillment

E. Ahaz tells Assyria of its treachery, weakening himself in the process

VI. Oracles Against the Nations

VII. Historical Account of King Hezekiah (Chapters 36–39)

A. Contrast with Ahaz – a case study of trust, not failed faith

1. "Double trouble" – threats expressed in letter
2. Hezekiah takes the situation to God
3. Motivation: so all will know you are the Lord (37:20)

B. A supernatural solution

C. Every problem is an invitation to faith

1. "Believing means entrusting oneself to a merciful love which always accepts and pardons. … Faith consists in the willingness to let ourselves be constantly transformed and renewed by God's call."[9]

VIII. Conclusion: Prayer of Renewal[10]

---

6 "An Exposition of the Orthodox Faith," 4:13.

7 Pope Benedict XVI, *Jesus of Nazareth: The Infancy Narratives,* (New York: Crown Publishing, 2012), 50.

8 Ibid, quoting Marius Reiser, *Bibelkritik,* 328.

9 *Lumen Fidei* 13.

10 For the text of this prayer, which is prayed at the close of each session, see page 12.

Session 5 – Questions

Isaiah Part 2 – Prophet of Consolation

A. Establish the Context

Isaiah's "Book of Woe" (Chapters 1–39) addressed the people of Judah during the Assyrian assault on Israel and Judah. He prophesied "woe" to all who opposed God and confronted the people of Judah with their failure to keep the covenant. He called them to return to the God who saved them from Egypt and lovingly raised them. When Israel was destroyed by Assyria, they saw the consequences of trusting in other gods. Even so, Ahaz and then Hezekiah turned to Egypt for help, which drew the Assyrian army to the gates of Jerusalem. Prompted by Hezekiah's prayers, God saved Jerusalem in a dramatic display of power, destroying Sennacherib's army without any human intervention. With such undeniable evidence of God's care, one might predict that Judah would return to him.

In Chapters 1–39, however, Isaiah does not offer us much hope of Judah's return to fidelity. He closes the "Book of Woe" with a cautionary incident in the life of Hezekiah. The king of faraway Babylon sends envoys and gifts after Hezekiah is cured. Hezekiah shows off all his treasures—an act that will foreshadow a future and more powerful Babylon, which will carry those treasures and God's people into captivity. In the first half of the book of Isaiah, there is little hope to cling to except the vision of the Holy One of Israel (Chapter 6) and the sign of the child and promised Messiah, "God with us" (Chapters 7 and 9).

In 587 BC, Babylon, under King Nebuchadnezzar, will have replaced Assyria as the dominant regional power and will destroy Jerusalem and the Temple and carry most of the remaining Judean population into exile.[1] Isaiah 40–66, often called the "Book of Consolation," is addressed to these exiles. In the words of Pope Francis, "The Lord is going to pour out over the Holy City and its inhabitants a 'cascade' of consolation, a veritable overflow of consolation. … 'As one whom his mother comforts, so I will comfort you'" (Isaiah 66:13).[2] This "cascade of tenderness" in the second half of the book of Isaiah promises the restoration of the nation and looks to the glorious future kingdom of God.

A final word about this session: Studying Isaiah 40–66 in a single session is like visiting Italy for the first time and trying to see everything in a single day. Not only does the text cover a lot of ground, it is filled with places of historical value, exquisite beauty, and deep spiritual meaning—all of which beg to be savored. Here, we find the Servant Songs and many passages used by the Gospel writers to describe Jesus and his life and mission.[3] And here, as in the "Book of Woe," we find the source of the lyrics of Handel's *Messiah*.[4] This session aims to give you the "big picture" of Isaiah's "Book of Consolation" by touching on a few highlights. We hope this will be just the start of the time you will spend savoring its bounty.

B. Read the Story

Before beginning the questions, read **Isaiah 40, 42, 44–45, and 63–66.** Do not worry if you do not understand everything; simply read to get a feel for Isaiah's "Book of Consolation." The following questions will take you for a deeper look at some of the highlights.

---

1 Two prior waves of deportation in 605 and 597 BC see the exile of the prophets Daniel, Baruch, and Ezekiel. We will follow Ezekiel and Daniel into that exile in future sessions.

2 Pope Francis homily, July 7, 2013.

3 Some of these and other messianic prophecies, along with New Testament references, can be found on the chart on pages 15-16.

4 See Isaiah 7:14, 9:2, 9:6, 11:1-5, 35:5-6, 40:9, 40:11, 53:3-6, 53:8, 60:2-3.

Going Deeper (optional): To get the entire story and message of Isaiah's "Book of Consolation," read **Isaiah 40–66.**

As always, pray before you read.

C. Take a Deeper Look

Answering these questions will draw you into the heart of the story. If you do not understand something, make a note of it to bring up in the small-group discussion.

"Comfort My People": Restoration Promised (Isaiah 40–41)

1. Recall that Isaiah begins in 1:2 with God's complaint against his rebellious sons. All through the years of Judah's rebellion and lack of repentance, God's message is "woe." Read **Isaiah 40:1-2.** Now that they are years into captivity, what is God's message to them?

2. From the time of the Exodus, God has promised to be with his people and to dwell among them. This is signified by his presence in the Holy of Holies in the Temple. In 587 BC, though, the Temple is destroyed. Now God's people are in exile, and they may wonder where he is. Read **Isaiah 40:3-11.** What good news is Isaiah asked to cry out to the people of Judah to bring them comfort?

3. a. For many generations, the people of Judah have witnessed firsthand the terrible power of nations that stand in defiance to God and against them. Read **Isaiah 40:12-31.** Who is the LORD, that they should listen to his call, let alone trust him and obey?

   b. In what ways have you experienced God's strength and support in your life? How do these verses speak to you?

4. **New Testament Connection:** There are sometimes "layers" of fulfillment to prophecies, each pointing to something beyond the last. The immediate fulfillment of Isaiah's prophecy will be when Judah is rescued from Babylon and allowed to return to the Promised Land of Israel. According to **Matthew 3:1-3,** to what future "rescue" and "return" do Isaiah's words point? Who will pick up the cry of the voice heard in Isaiah 40:3?

"Behold My Servant": Agents of Restoration (Isaiah 42–55)

In Isaiah 41:8, God's people (both Israel and Judah) are called God's "chosen" servant. They have been created to be God's witnesses to the nations—yet, by turning their hearts from God, they have become spiritually blind and deaf and are no longer capable of bearing his message (42:18-20, 43:8-10). In fulfillment of his promise, God chooses to redeem them by sending another Servant (Chapters 42–55). This Servant is the subject of four "Servant Songs" that progressively reveal the Servant's character and mission.

5. In the following chart, read each of the four Servant Songs, and record what you learn about the Servant's identity, character, and mission.

Servant Song in Isaiah	The Servant's Identity and Character	The Servant's Mission
42:1-4		
49:1-6		
50:4-9		
52:13–53:12		

6. Each of the Servant Songs is followed by a kind of unfolding or expansion of the song, like a commentary. These verses speak of the effects or significance of the Servant's work. Read the following passages along with the comments you made above and write what you learn from the commentary verses.

Servant Song "Commentary" in Isaiah	The Significance or Results of the Servant's Work
42:5-20	
49:7-13	
50:10-11	
54:1-17	

7. Reading these Servant Songs in the bright light of the Cross, it is not hard to see the face of Christ. Yet, like many prophecies, they have both an immediate and a future fulfillment. We will look first at the temporal restoration promised to Judah and the immediate "servant" God sends to perform it.

   a. In Isaiah 43, God promises to overthrow Babylon, free his people, and restore them to their land. He then names the person who will enable them to return in Isaiah 44:28. What is his name, and what specific task will he be given?

   b. Read **Isaiah 45:1-7.** For whose sake will God help this pagan ruler overthrow Babylon, and for what purpose?

Cyrus is called God's "shepherd" in 44:28 and his "anointed" in 45:1. Both of these titles are significant. The rulers of God's people are called "shepherds," and Psalm 23 refers to the LORD as "Shepherd." "Anointed One" is the English equivalent of the Hebrew "Messiah," and it has normally been reserved for the God-anointed king in David's royal line, although priests (and sometimes prophets) were also anointed. In the present context, it means one chosen by God to fulfill a particular task. Either of these titles applied to a pagan king like Cyrus would be offensive to the people of Israel. Yet, Isaiah makes it clear that God is God over all of the kingdoms of the earth (44:6, 24). Cyrus acts only under the sovereign command of the LORD and to carry out his purposes. Jesus makes this concept clear in his words to Pontius Pilate in John 19:11a: "You would have no power over me unless it had been given you from above."

8. **New Testament Connection:** As wonderful as the hope of a political redemption through Cyrus must have been, Isaiah gives a much more profound hope—of a spiritual Redeemer who will free all people from the grip of sin by taking on the punishment due them. Who is the "real," or ultimate, Redeemer-Servant to whom Cyrus points? Read **Acts 8:30-38.**

   a. What part of Isaiah is quoted here? *Isaiah 53:* ________

   b. How does Philip interpret this passage?

   c. Read **Isaiah 53:4-7.** How are some of the details fulfilled in Jesus Christ, according to the following New Testament verses? Make a note of which verses in Isaiah 53 provided your answers.

   Matthew 27:12-14:

   John 1:29:

   1 Peter 2:23-25:

   Romans 5:8:

"Arise, Shine; for Your Light Has Come": Zion Restored (Isaiah 56–66)

For the remainder of Isaiah, the focus shifts to encompass not only the return of Judah to the land, but to a even more distant fulfillment—the "New Jerusalem," the final destiny of God's people and the Church as it is intended to be for eternity. Because of this, Chapters 56–66 have particular meaning for us, God's people, who belong to the kingdom established by the ultimate Suffering Servant, Jesus, yet who wait for the final establishment of that kingdom at his second coming.

9. Earlier we saw the figures of Cyrus and of the Servant, chosen and sent to redeem.

   a. Now read **Isaiah 59:15b-21,** and describe the messianic figure pictured there. What is his mission?

   b. Read **Isaiah 61:1-7.** What additional details does this tell us about the mission of the LORD's coming Anointed One?

10. Read **Isaiah 65:17-25.** Based on this passage, how would you describe the promised new creation, the New Jerusalem?

11. **New Testament Connection:** Read **Revelation 21:1-5,** in which John is given a vision of a new heaven and new earth and of the arrival of the New Jerusalem. How does John's vision fulfill Isaiah's prophecy?

D. Application

This question will help you apply one of the key themes of the session to your life. After meditating on it, respond to God with a brief written prayer if you choose.

Do you ever feel like you are away from God, like you cannot feel his presence? Do you ever feel forsaken or desolate? Review your notes about the Servant Songs and commentaries (questions 5 and 6). Choose the one that means the most to you and read it again. What consolation does it offer?

Dear Lord …

Session 5 Talk Notes

Isaiah Part 2 – Prophet of Consolation

I. Setting the Stage

A. Background

B. "To comfort the afflicted"

C. Revealing the Messiah (blended layers of prophecy)

II. Major Themes

A. The Holy One of Israel is in control

B. Promises of return, restoration, new creation

1. Words of comfort (40:1-2)
2. Your warfare has ended (*avodah* = "service")
3. A voice in the wilderness (verses 3-4)
   a. Prophetic promise of return
   b. Something missing; multi-layered fulfillment
   c. New Testament fulfillment in John the Baptist – a future, deeper Exodus
   d. Herald of Good News (Gk., *euangelium;* verses 9-11)
      i. God himself will come with might to feed, lead, gather
      ii. Challenge to wait on God's promises

C. The promise of the Messiah

1. Four Servant Songs – "snapshots of the Savior," who will:
   a. Bring justice (Isaiah 42:1-4)
   b. Lead a new Exodus; be a light to the nations (Isaiah 49:1-6)
   c. Bring a word to the weary; suffer (Isaiah 50:4-9)
   d. Suffer, take away sin and guilt, bear judgment, be vindicated by God (Isaiah 52:13–53:12)
2. Putting the pieces together
   a. May describe the people in exile, even Isaiah
   b. In hindsight, all the pieces come together in Jesus

III. The Suffering Servant Songs Point to Jesus (Songs I and IV)

A. Isaiah 42:1-4, "Behold my servant" (first Servant Song)

1. Foreshadows Jesus' baptism (Matthew 3:17; John 1:33)
   a. "I will put my Spirit upon him"
   b. He will bring forth justice to the nations
   c. The lamb

2. "Commentary" verses 5-17: "I have given you [the servant] as a covenant to the people" (verse 6)
    a. Gives new meaning to the Last Supper and the Mass
        i. Jesus identifies himself with the New Covenant
        ii. The Servant will heal (verses 7-9)
        – "Justice" – *mishpat* (king initiating a jubilee)
        – He will make all things new
    b. Their response – Sing to the Lord a new song (Revelation 5, 15)

B. Isaiah 52:13–53:12, the Suffering Servant (fourth Servant Song)
1. Quoted at least seven times in New Testament
    a. Gospels
    b. Stephen's sermon (Acts 7)
    c. Ethiopian eunuch
    d. Paul — two times in Romans
    e. 1 Peter 2, suffering of Church united to Jesus' suffering
2. Five parts, three verses each; climax in the middle (Isaiah 53:5)
    a. Describes the Passion
    b. He "was" bruised – seems past tense (in Septuagint translation, changed to future tense)
    c. A word still "in waiting" – anticipates something yet unfilled
3. Substitutionary suffering
4. He shall see the fruit of his suffering: our salvation (verse 10; see Hebrews 12:12)

IV. The Victory Applied (Isaiah 54–55)

A. Chapter 54 for Zion

B. Chapter 55 for the world

V. A Vision of the Church, the New Israel of God (Isaiah 56–66)

A. A unique section; different focus and feel
1. A "third Isaiah"?
2. Looks to the future, to the New Israel of God

B. "Gap" between first coming of Messiah and final coming of Christ: a call to faithful waiting

C. The Our Father, a prayer of waiting and working for the kingdom here and yet to come
1. Isaiah 63 and 64 – first time God invoked as "our" Father

D. Isaiah closes on a high note (66:10-13)
1. The New Israel of God drawn from all the nations
2. Rejoicing and consolation

VI. Conclusion: Prayer of Renewal[5]

[5] For the text of this prayer, which is prayed at the close of each session, see page 12.

Session 6 – Questions

Jeremiah – The Broken-Hearted Prophet

A. Establish the Context

In the previous session, we explored Isaiah's words of hope to the exiles following the destruction of the Temple and the holy city of Jerusalem. We also saw how these same words provide hope to us today as we await the "new heavens and a new earth" (Isaiah 65:17). In this session, we are taken to "ground level" to witness the events leading up to the Babylonian exile and the destruction of Jerusalem through the experience of an eyewitness, Jeremiah. Jeremiah's ministry spans more than four decades, from 627 BC until about 580 BC. (Locate this period on your *Bible Timeline* Chart.) It is a volatile time, as the regional powers of Assyria, Egypt, and Babylon fight for domination, and the fragile kingdom of Judah struggles to survive in the middle. Repeated attempts by the kingdom of Judah to ally itself with Egypt in hopes of escaping Babylonian rule will bring down a series of crippling attacks from the northern superpower, each ending in the deportation of more people to Babylon (see the three blue arrows on your Chart). The last expulsion in 587 BC will be painfully united to the final ruination of Jerusalem, the Temple, and the Davidic throne.

In the decades prior to these events, Jeremiah faithfully conveys God's Word to the people, to the religious authorities, and to the kings who reign over Judah during this time. Despite Jeremiah's warnings, the people rest dangerously on the false hope that God will never allow the Temple to be destroyed. They may have ears, but they refuse to hear God's Word. Jeremiah is rejected by his own people, even threatened with death. Yet he cannot remain silent. He says that God's Word is like "a burning fire shut up in my bones" (20:9).

Given all of this, it is not surprising that Jeremiah is remembered as the "weeping prophet." His suffering and rejection begin to embody the Suffering Servant of Isaiah and foreshadow the fulfillment of Isaiah's prophecy in the person of Jesus Christ. Despite the dark days that Jeremiah lives through, he is also a prophet of hope. Like the prophets before him, he enacts living parables that become signs of restoration. From jail, as Jerusalem is surrounded and its destruction is certain, Jeremiah is instructed by God to purchase some real estate. This is after he has predicted a seventy-year exile! With this purchase comes a prophecy: "For thus says the LORD of hosts, the God of Israel: Houses and fields and vineyards shall again be bought on this land" (Jeremiah 32:15). Jeremiah's purchase is a supreme act of hope for Judah. It is the end of an era, but not the end of the story.

The chapters of Jeremiah are not arranged chronologically. Instead, narrative and historic sections are mixed with oracles and prophetic poems that offer a window into Jeremiah's heart and soul.

The following chart shows where key events in Jeremiah's life and ministry fall in relation to historic events and the reigns of the kings of Judah. (Locate the kings on your *Bible Timeline* Chart.)

Timeline (BC) and Ruling King of Judah	Verses in Jeremiah that take place during each king's reign
640–609 – Josiah	1:1-19 3:6–6:30
609 – Jehoahaz 609–598 – Jehoiakim	7:1-34 25:1–26:24 35:1–36:32 45:1–48:47
598–597 – Jehoiachin (Jeconiah) 597–586 – Zedekiah	20:1–22:30 24:1-10 27:1–33:22 37:1–39:18 49:1–52:34
587ff – After the exile of Zedekiah and destruction of the Temple	40:1–44:30, 52:1-34

B. Read the Story

In order to get the historical context, begin by reading **2 Kings 22–24.** Then read **Jeremiah 1-2, 7, 29:1-14, and 31-33** to get a feel for the prophet's message. Locate Jeremiah on your *Bible Timeline* Chart.

Going Deeper (optional): To get the entire story and message of this prophet, read the entire book of **Jeremiah.** The following outline may help you keep your bearings.

Chapters 1–10	Warning of judgment due to the broken covenant
Chapters 11–29	Jeremiah's struggles
Chapters 30–33	Jeremiah's "Book of Consolation"; the New Covenant to come and future restoration for Judah and Israel
Chapters 34–45	Judgment on Judah
Chapters 46–51	Judgment on the nations
Chapter 52	Conclusion: the fall of Jerusalem and exile

As always, pray before you read.

C. Take a Deeper Look

Answering these questions will draw you into the heart of the story. If you do not understand something, make a note of it to bring up in the small-group discussion.

Kings of Judah in the Time of Jeremiah (2 Kings 22–24)

1. It has been nearly a century since Israel's fall to Assyria, and Samaria is under foreign control. Jeremiah preaches to Judah, the Southern Kingdom, during the reigns of kings Josiah, Jehoiakim, and Zedekiah. Locate them on your *Bible Timeline* Chart; then read the following and record briefly what you learn about their reigns.

    a. Josiah – Judah's last faithful king

    2 Kings 22:1-2:

    2 Kings 23:1-5, 21-30 (after Josiah has the Temple repaired and the book of the Law is found in it):

    b. Jehoiakim

    2 Kings 23:34-37:

    2 Kings 24:1-2:

    c. Zedekiah

    2 Kings 24:17–25:12:

Jeremiah's Call and Message (Jeremiah 1–2)

2. Chapter 1 tells how Jeremiah is called to be a prophet. Read **Jeremiah 1:1-5.**

    a. What four things does God tell Jeremiah about his calling?

    b. Compare this to **Isaiah 44:1-2 and 49:1-6** (the call of the servant) and **Galatians 1:15-16** (the call of St. Paul). What do they have in common?

3. Read **Jeremiah 1:7-9.** Jeremiah's initial response is to object on the basis of his youth and ignorance. How does God reply?

4. In **Jeremiah 1:10, 15-19,** God outlines Jeremiah's job description and the challenges he will face. What are the two opposite aspects of his role, and how will God help him accomplish them?

5. In the following passages, what does Jeremiah's response in prayer to difficult circumstances reveal about the struggle within his heart?

   Jeremiah 17:14-18:

   Jeremiah 20:7-18:

6. In Jeremiah 2, the prophet is called to plead for repentance in the streets of Jerusalem.

   a. Read **2:9-13.** What are the two great evils that Judah is charged with? Explain the metaphor Jeremiah uses to make them clear.

   b. What are some of the leaky, inadequate "cisterns" we try to use to replace God in our lives?

Jeremiah in the Temple

The people of Judah see the Temple in Jerusalem as their "ace in the hole"; since God is present there, they count on it as a type of magical protection against any and all enemies. They place their trust, then, in a building made of stone, rather than on a life built on covenant faithfulness. As we will see, their trust is misplaced.

7. Read **Jeremiah 7.**

   a. What are some of the sins of Judah that are outlined here?

b. The people of Judah may think Israel is destroyed only because it lacks the protection of the Temple. What historical event does Jeremiah recall to illustrate the folly of their belief? (See **verses 12-15.**)

8. **New Testament Connection:** Read **Matthew 21:12-13,** where Jesus quotes both Isaiah 56:7 and Jeremiah 7:11. How does the context of the quote from Jeremiah give deeper meaning to Jesus' words? (Read also **CCC 584.**)

A Future and a Hope (Jeremiah 29–33)

In the course of his reign, King Jehoiakim wavers in his alliance between Egypt and Babylon with the result that twice Babylon invades Judah and takes captives to Babylon: first in 605 BC and then in 597 BC. Jehoiakim dies before facing this second invasion, and his son Jehoiachin is left to bear the brunt of his actions. After reigning for just three months, Jehoiachin (also known as Jeconiah; see Matthew 1:12), the Queen Mother, his officials, and all but the poorest people are taken into exile. In addition, all the treasures of the Temple and the palace are taken away.

9. During this time, false prophets fill the air with claims that the exiles will be home soon from Babylon and all will be well. God sends a different message to the exiles through Jeremiah. Read **Jeremiah 29:1-14** before going on. (In the RSV-CE, "Jeconiah" in verse 2 is another name for Jehoiachin.)

   a. How are the exiles to live? Why? (See **verses 4-9.**)

   b. The "why" of God's instructions becomes clearer in verses 10-14. What hope does he give them?

10. Like Isaiah, Jeremiah has a "Book of Consolation." Chapters 30–33 are the "heart" of Jeremiah, full of beautiful words of restoration and hope, speaking of future days alluded to in Jeremiah's call—when, after uprooting and breaking down, God will watch over, build, and plant his people once again (see **1:10 and 31:28**).

    God is faithful to his covenant promise, but how can God be faithful given that his people have broken the covenant? Read **Jeremiah 31:31-37.**

a. Explain what God will do for his people (verses 31-34).

b. How sure is this promise (verses 35-37)?

11. This promised "New Covenant" is something truly new. No amount of animal blood can atone for the sins of Israel. The breaking of the covenant requires the death of one of the parties. In God's mercy, he will send his own Son to take on Israel's sins—to become Israel, the Suffering Servant of Isaiah, in order to atone for its sins.[1]

    Read the following passages, and explain what you learn about this "New Covenant" foretold by Jeremiah.

    Luke 22:19-20:

    CCC 781:

    CCC 613:

    CCC 1965:

D. Application

This question will help you apply one of the key themes of the session to your life. After meditating on it, respond to God with a brief written prayer if you choose.

We have seen into Jeremiah's heart in the way he prays in the midst of difficult and confusing circumstances. What about God's designs do you find hard to understand? Is there something you are going through that you think is difficult to bring to God in prayer? Choose one of Jeremiah's prayers from question 5. Rewrite it below to fit your situation, and offer it up to the Father.

Dear Lord …

[1] See Romans 9:15-22.

Session 6 Talk Notes

Jeremiah – The Broken-Hearted Prophet

I. Setting the Stage

A. Background

B. "The weeping prophet"

1. At deafness of people

2. Jeremiah drawn into the pathos of God, experiences rejection

3. Commanded not to marry as a visible sign of their loss

4. Baruch – Jeremiah's secretary

II. The Call of Jeremiah (Chapter 1)

A. Three verbs describe God's work with Jeremiah

1. Known *(yadah)* before he was formed in womb

   a. Intimate knowledge

   b. Present tense indicates instantaneous, complete knowing

2. Consecrated (*qadash,* "to set apart, make holy")

3. Appointed

   a. Jonah – God appointed the whale

   b. Commissioned with a mission

4. All these are true of us

5. These give confidence

B. Jeremiah's "job description" (1:9-10, 18)

1. God's words in his mouth

2. Set against nations … to pluck up and break down

3. I will make you "a fortified city" against the land (verse 18)

4. "Be not afraid," "I am with you" ("bookends" verses 8, 19)

III. Charges Against the People (Chapter 2)

A. Broken covenant, idolatry, injustice, hollow religion

B. Bride-bridegroom language (verses 1-3)

C. Analogy of the cistern (verse 13) – two great evils

1. They have forsaken God, the fountain of living water

2. They have built broken cisterns that hold no water

a. Idolizing themselves and the work of their hands

b. Seeking to fill the void in life. Pope Francis:[2]

i. "The opposite of faith is … idolatry"

ii. "Idols exist … as a pretext for setting ourselves at the center of reality and worshiping the work of our own hands. Once man has lost the fundamental orientation [toward God] which unifies his existence, he breaks down into the multiplicity of his desires"

c. *Diabolos,* diabolical ("to scatter")

d. In contrast, God brings wholeness, integrity

i. *Shalom,* "nothing missing, nothing broken"

e. Result: ever thirsting, never satisfied

f. A call to spiritual vigilance

D. The people presume on the Temple for protection (Chapter 7)

1. Fail to understand need for covenant faithfulness

2. Violate commandments while expecting deliverance (verses 9-10)

3. The Temple has "become a den of robbers" (verse 11)

a. Quoted by Jesus (Matthew 21:13)

---

2 *Lumen Fidei* 13.

   b. Jesus unites this with Isaiah 56:7, the Temple as a house of prayer for the nations

   c. Jesus cleanses the Temple: a prophetic sign of what will happen to it because of their infidelity

E. Burning children in sacrifice (7:30-31)

   1. Hinnom Valley – later a burning garbage dump, "Gehenna"

   2. Analogy of eternal separation from God

F. The people ignore Jeremiah's warnings, destruction is assured

IV. From Destruction, Comes Hope

A. Jeremiah's "Book of Consolation" (Chapters 30–33)

B. A letter to the exiles: God has a "return policy" (29:10-14)

C. Joy in future return (31:13)

D. Prediction of messianic age, New Covenant (31:31-33)

   1. Israel and Judah together

   2. Law on hearts, not on stone

   3. I will be their God, they will be my people

E. The New Covenant is Jesus (recall Isaiah 42)

   1. Pope Benedict XVI – hope as the distinguishing mark of Christians[3]

F. Jeremiah purchases property: a sign of hope (Chapter 32)

   1. However bad it looks, God has a plan

   2. The Eucharist as a pledge of our hope

V. Conclusion: Prayer of Renewal[4]

[3] Benedict XVI, *Spe Salvi* 2.

[4] For the text of this prayer, which is prayed at the close of each session, see page 12.

Prophets of the Exile (722–538 BC)
Introduction to Sessions 7-8

The Divided Kingdom came to an end for the Northern Kingdom (Israel) in 722 BC because Israel failed to heed God's plea through the prophets to return to him and his covenant. As we have seen, Israel was conquered by Assyria. Most of the people were taken into exile. They were resettled among other nations conquered by Assyria, and populations from those nations were moved into Israel. Although Judah remained intact in the south, the ten tribes of Israel in the north were no more.

Eventually, Assyria was conquered by Babylon. Under King Nebuchadnezzar, Babylon deported many of the residents of Judah in three waves starting in 605 BC. The third (and final) deportation in 587 BC was marked by destruction of Jerusalem and the Temple.

Both the exile of Israel and the Babylonian captivity of Judah had been foretold by the prophets who warned the people of the consequence of turning their hearts from God. **Now, God sends prophets to speak to the people of Judah in captivity.** Find Daniel, Baruch, and Ezekiel on *The Bible Timeline* Chart in the baby blue period of the Exile, at the top of the blue arrows representing the three deportations of Judah.

We will spend two sessions in the time of the Exile studying Ezekiel and Daniel.

Session 7 – Questions

Ezekiel – God's Watchman on the Wall

A. Establish the Context

The first prophet we will study from the period of the Exile is Ezekiel.

In the last session, we saw that in 597 BC, the Babylonian king Nebuchadnezzar swept down into Judah. Replacing King Jehoiachin with his uncle Mattaniah (renamed Zedekiah), he deported Jehoiachin to Babylon along with the Queen Mother and the best and brightest of the population. Many of these, one assumes, were the very people, priests, and leaders who rejected Jeremiah's pleas to repent, people who trusted in the existence of the Temple while ignoring what it signified—the presence of God with his people in covenant relationship with them. They, like so many, did not know the LORD.

Jeremiah, who is allowed to remain at home, continues to write to the Judeans exiled in Babylon. He insists that in spite of what certain false prophets have claimed, God himself has sent them into exile. While many might not believe it, Jerusalem will be destroyed, and their exile will be long—seventy years long, in fact. In time, God will begin the process of restoration: "For I know the plans I have for you, says the LORD, plans for welfare and not for evil, to give you a future and a hope" (Jeremiah 29:11).

This may have been hard for the people to believe. According to Benedict XVI, the fact that both the land and the Temple had been lost was "incomprehensible … a God who could not defend his worshipers and his worship was seen to be, at the time, a weak God. Indeed, he was no God at all; he had abandoned his divinity. And so, being driven out of their own land … [was] a terrible trial: Has our God been vanquished, and is our faith void?"[1]

There are three "waves" of exile to Babylon, culminating in 587 BC with the destruction of the Temple. Among those exiled in the second wave is a young priest named Ezekiel, whose name means "God strengthens." True to his name, he is strengthened to speak to the other exiles even though they do not want to hear, and he bears witness to the God who is not confined to a particular piece of land, but who, as Benedict XVI continues, "could drive his faithless people into another land in order to make himself known there."[2] Ezekiel bears witness to the God who gives renewed strength to his weakened people even in exile.

While Jeremiah utters his prophetic message from Jerusalem, Ezekiel prophesies from exile in Babylon. His visions and messages are larger than life, even bizarre. He uses apocalyptic language to describe what he sees and to convey his message. Perhaps he believes he must shout and startle those who are deaf and blind to God to get their attention. Given the people's loss of the knowledge of God, it should not surprise us that Ezekiel's prophecy is marked by dramatic visions revealing God's glory and presence—or that the phrase, "Then you will know that I am the LORD" (7:4) tolls like a bell throughout the book.[3]

---

1 Joseph Ratzinger (Pope Benedict XVI). *'In the Beginning …': A Catholic Understanding of the Story of Creation and the Fall* (Grand Rapids, MI: Wm. B. Eerdmans, 1995), 11.

2 Ibid.

3 See Ezekiel 7:4, 28:23, 24, 26, 29:6, 16, 21, and 32:15.

B. Read the Story

Read **Ezekiel 1–3, 11:14-25, 34, 43:1-17, and 47:1-12** before you answer the questions. (At this point, read to get a feel for the book, not to understand it fully.) Next, locate Ezekiel on your *Bible Timeline* Chart, paying attention to the time period and pertinent events during that time, to the king (or kings) who reigned during his time, and when and to whom he is speaking.

Going Deeper (optional): To get the full story and message of this prophet, read the entire book of **Ezekiel.**

As always, pray before you read.

C. Take a Deeper Look

Answering these questions will draw you into the heart of the story. If you do not understand something, make a note of it to bring up in the small-group discussion.

Ezekiel's Call and Ministry (Ezekiel 1–3)

Psalm 137 captures the lament of the exiles: "By the waters of Babylon, there we sat down and wept, when we remembered Zion. On the willows there we hung up our lyres. For there our captors required of us songs. … How shall we sing the LORD's song in a foreign land?" (verses 1-4). Let that image set the scene for Ezekiel, who we meet by a river in Babylon (called here "the land of the Chaldeans").

1. Read **Ezekiel 1.** Here, the prophet describes how the Word of the LORD came to him in a strange and glorious vision. This is not an easy read. Even the great Church Father and Scripture scholar St. Jerome found Ezekiel to be a puzzle. Try not to get caught up in the details of the vision; simply read for the general sense of it.

   a. Where is Ezekiel? Where is the throne in Ezekiel's vision?

   b. **Think About It:** What is the significance of this, as compared to the location of the throne in Isaiah's vision? (See **Isaiah 6:1-4** and "Establish the Context" on page 59.)

2. a. Given the charge brought by several of the prophets that the people do not know the LORD, this vision may be as important for the people to read as it is for Ezekiel to witness. What might they learn about God from Ezekiel 1?

b. **Think About It:** Today it might be hard to imagine God as tied to a particular physical country. But do we perhaps live as though he is confined to our churches? Comment on this. What application does Ezekiel 1 have for you?

The Meaning of "Son of Man"

God does not address Ezekiel by name in these visions, but niney-three times the prophet is called "son of man" (in Hebrew, *ben-'adam*). Jesus will later apply this title to himself. Here in Ezekiel, however, the phrase does not have messianic overtones. Rather, it identifies Ezekiel as a human being, highlighting his creaturely standing and contrasting him with the almighty and glorious Yahweh.

3. Read **Ezekiel 2:1–3:11,** in which the Spirit enters Ezekiel and commissions him to speak on his behalf to "a nation of rebels" (2:3), "impudent and stubborn" (2:4); a rebellious house who may well refuse to listen to him. What is the scroll he is given, and what is the significance of having Ezekiel eat it?

4. Read **Ezekiel 3:12-21.** What does it mean that God makes Ezekiel a "watchman" (verse 17) for the house of Israel? How critical is it for him to do his job?

Judgment on Jerusalem (Ezekiel 4–24)

Ezekiel is made to identify with God's message, sometimes in dramatic ways. The Lord strikes him dumb until Jerusalem falls, only allowing him to speak when he has a direct message to relay. At other times, he is to embody his message through his actions. For example, Ezekiel is told to build a model of Jerusalem and symbolically enact the siege that will come against it. He is also told to illustrate Jerusalem's destruction by burning, striking, and scattering his own shaved hair. "This is Jerusalem," God says (5:5)—then details its fate.[4]

[4] See Ezekiel 5:12: "A third part of you shall die of pestilence and be consumed in the famine in the midst of you; a third part shall fall by the sword round about you; and a third part I will scatter to all the winds and will unsheathe the sword after them."

5. The prophets speak of a "day of the LORD"[5]—not a single day, but a final day of reckoning, when God's glory and power will be revealed. Read **Ezekiel 7:2-3, 5-7, 10, 12-13.** What "has come" to Jerusalem?

6. a. One year and one month after the chariot vision (592 BC, five years before the fall of Jerusalem) Ezekiel is transported to Jerusalem in a vision and shown terrible atrocities: idols standing in the Temple itself; elders, convinced the LORD does not see them, burning incense to idols there; and men with their backs to the Temple (the ultimate insult), worshiping the sun toward the east (Chapter 8). God calls on six divine "executioners" in Chapter 9 to deliver his wrath to the city. Before sending them to do their deadly work, what does God ask? (Read **Ezekiel 9:3-6.**)

   b. ***Catechism* Connection:** Read **CCC 1296.** What do these Old Testament "marks" prefigure in the New Covenant today?

7. In Chapter 10, wheeled cherubim like those in Chapter 1 appear over the court of the Temple. Read **Ezekiel 10:3-4, 10:18-19, and 11:22-23.** Trace the movement of the glory of the LORD, and comment on its significance.

Future Restoration (Ezekiel 33–48)

Eventually the time comes for God to act (24:14). Ezekiel's wife dies suddenly, a sign that the Temple—the delight of Israel—will be profaned and many of those left behind in Jerusalem will die. But the "day of the LORD" involves not just wrath but a promise of restoration. Several times, God says he will take initiative: that "he himself" will remember his covenant and establish an everlasting one which promises the forgiveness of sins (16:60-63);[6] he will give them a new heart and spirit (11:19, 36:26); he will replant them in the land (17:22ff); and perhaps most beautifully, he will search for and shepherd his people.

[5] See Isaiah 13:6, 9 and 58:13; Jeremiah 46:10; Ezekiel 13:5 and 30:3; Joel 1:15, 2:1, 11, 31 and 3:14; Amos 5:18, 20; Obadiah 1:15; Zephaniah 1:7, 8, 14; Zechariah 14:1; Malachi 4:5.

[6] This is the same promise God spoke through Jeremiah in Jerusalem (Jeremiah 31:31-34).

8. Read **Ezekiel 34.**

   a. Who are the shepherds addressed in verses 1-10, and what charge does the LORD make against them?

   b. What will God do for his sheep, according to verses 11-16?

   c. In verses 23-24, there is a transition from "I myself" (the shepherd in verse 15) to another who will shepherd the sheep. Who is it? Describe him.

9. **New Testament Connection:** Read the following passages from John's Gospel and answer the questions.

   John 10:11-18: How does Jesus resolve this dilemma between God and his "servant David" shepherding his sheep? (See also **CCC 754.**)

   John 6:51-58: If Jesus is the Good Shepherd described by Ezekiel, how does he feed his flock?

10. God's restoration of Israel will go far beyond returning the people to the land. Their exile is a reflection of their self imposed, internal "exile" from communion with God. A true return will need to be effected internally as well. Read **Ezekiel 36:22-27.** What does God promise, and why?

Ezekiel 37 contains an unforgettable picture of the promised restoration: a valley of dry, dead bones brought to life and filled with the living Spirit of God. The word *ruah* (breath, wind, spirit) is used ten times in the chapter (four times in verse 9 alone). This same breath brought life to the dust that became Adam and will fill the disciples with the Holy Spirit at Pentecost. This same animating power is given to us in the sacraments.

11. Fourteen years after the conquest of Jerusalem, Ezekiel is granted a vision in which a future, restored Temple is revealed and measured.

    a. Read **Ezekiel 43:1-7.** What does he see, and what is he told?

    b. In Chapter 47, Ezekiel describes the life-giving, healing waters pouring forth from the Temple.[7] The renewed Temple will be at the heart of the renewed land of Israel and a renewed Jerusalem. What will be the name of the city? (See **48:35.**)

12. God's beautiful promise of a new, indwelling Spirit has been fulfilled at Pentecost, and all the baptized now receive this marvelous gift. Read **CCC 736 and 1432.** What about God's gift of a new heart and spirit, as explained here, particularly speaks to you, and why?

D. Application

This question will help you apply one of the key themes of the session to your life. After meditating on it, respond to God with a brief written prayer if you choose.

Do you or your parish feel dry or lifeless like the dry bones in Ezekiel 37? Read that chapter again, and consider how you can you take hope from that vision and its revelation of the power of God.

Dear Lord …

[7] For further study, compare Ezekiel's Temple vision with John's vision of the New Jerusalem in Revelation 21–22, and see John's use of this imagery in John 7:37-39, 19:34.

Session 7 Talk Notes

Ezekiel – God's Watchman on the Wall

I. Setting the Stage

A. Background

1. Place on *Bible Timeline* Chart

2. Audience

B. Relevance to today

C. Command to write what he sees

II. Ezekiel's Vision (Chapter 1)

A. Time – "the thirtieth year" (verse 1)

B. Place – "the land of the Chaldeans by the river Chebar" (verse 3)

1. Psalm 137

2. Their circumstances

C. Vision of God's throne

1. Striking images reveal God's glory (*kavod:* "heavy")

2. Ezekiel's response (1:28) compared to Isaiah 6

3. Significance of chariot

a. God present with them
b. Power, glory extend throughout earth
c. God a "sanctuary" to them (11:16)

4. Purpose of the vision

III. Ezekiel's Task and Message

A. Combat denial; Jerusalem's destruction inevitable

B. Call to repentance, conversion

C. He is a "watchman on the wall"

D. Wake them up to their spiritual distance

E. Warning through words and symbolic actions

IV. Vision of the Jerusalem Temple (Chapter 8)

A. The glory of the Lord

B. Abominations, idolatry

C. The faithful remnant marked with a sign (Chapter 9)

1. The *tau*

2. Power in signs

3. Signs of belonging and God's presence in the world

D. The glory of the Lord departs (Chapters 10, 11)

1. Lament over their unfaithfulness

2. Compare Jesus weeping over Jerusalem (Matthew 23:37; Luke 13:34)

V. The Fall of Jerusalem and the Temple (Chapter 24)

A. Ezekiel's wife dies as the Temple falls

VI. Ezekiel's "Book of Consolation"

A. Words of hope after fall of Jerusalem

B. Rebuke on the wicked shepherds of Judah (Chapter 34)

1. Promise that God himself will shepherd his sheep (verses 11-16)

2. Jesus attributes these words to himself

C. Promise of new heart and spirit; hearts of flesh in place of stone (36:26)

1. Fulfilled first at Pentecost

2. Gift given at baptism, confirmation, Eucharist: God's Spirit in us

3. *Ezekiel* means "to be strengthened by God"

4. His mission is ours

VII. Conclusion: Prayer of Renewal[8]

8 For the text of this prayer, which is prayed at the close of each session, see page 12.

A. Establish the Context

Ezekiel's hopeful visions of God's glory and continuing presence came at a crucial time in Israel's history: the painful years surrounding the destruction of Jerusalem. During this time, the exiled remnant of Judah had to acclimate to the realities of separation. Israel was originally twelve tribes inhabiting the Promised Land and ruled by a descendant of David from Jerusalem. Not one of these markers of their covenant identity remained after 587 BC. Ezekiel's visions and promises aside, the people have a long road ahead of them—seventy years of exile, as Jeremiah foretold. And they are living in the lap of an empire that must seem like a beast: ruthless, demanding, and voracious; crushing and absorbing all opponents. It would be easy to doubt the "I AM" and pay allegiance instead to Babylon. How will the people of Judah muster the scraps of faith that remain and hold strong until the promised restoration? And even after that—how will they live out their faith under continued foreign domination?

The answer to those questions and a stellar example can be found in the Book of Daniel. Taken into captivity as a teenager with the first wave of exiles in 605 BC, this faithful young man rises to power in the court of King Nebuchadnezzar and remains through the reigns of Belshazzar and Darius the Mede.[1] Daniel lives long enough to see the rise of Cyrus the Persian, who will send exiles home to rebuild Jerusalem. From youth to old age, his life bears dramatic witness to the way God protects those who are faithful in trial. And the events of his life and the visions he is granted send the strong message that in spite of appearances, God has everything under control. He can be trusted because the nations that oppose him will be put down, one after the other, until only God's kingdom and justice remain.

The book of Daniel is an unusual text on several counts. Unlike the prophets before him, Daniel does not speak the "Word of the LORD" to the people of his day. Like them, though, he speaks prophetically of things to come. He also speaks of the future bodily resurrection of God's people—a complement to Ezekiel's "valley of bones," but also the most specific description of God's plan for the human body to this point in the Old Testament.

For this and other reasons, Daniel has been connected to both the wisdom tradition and the prophetic tradition. Therefore, Daniel is listed with the "Writings" in the Hebrew canon[2] rather than among the prophets, while the Greek version of the Old Testament, the Septuagint, places Daniel between the major and minor prophets. This placement is followed by Christian Bibles. While most of the book is written in Hebrew, Daniel 2:4–7:28 is written in Aramaic. In addition, some portions are in Greek,[3] which are included in the Septuagint version of Daniel and can be found in Catholic but not Protestant versions of the Bible. As for the dating of the book, many scholars argue for authorship in the second century BC during the time of the Maccabees, while others provide support for the traditional dating four centuries earlier, in its historical setting.

---

[1] While Daniel, Josephus, and ancient Jewish commentaries mention King Darius, this royal figure is absent from Babylonian historical accounts. Scholars are still debating his identity.

[2] The "Writings" also include 1 and 2 Chronicles, Ezra, Nehemiah, Job, Psalms, Proverbs, Ecclesiastes, Lamentations, Song of Songs, Ruth, and Esther.

[3] The Greek portions include a long prayer inserted in Chapter 3 as well as all of Chapters 13 and 14.

Daniel can be divided into three parts.

Chapters 1–6	*Narrative* (the story of Daniel and his three fellow captives in Babylon)
Chapters 7–12	*Apocalyptic* (four visions that reveal the sweep of history from God's perspective)
Chapters 13–14	*Narrative* (more stories of Daniel from the Septuagint version that are not included in the later Hebrew canon)

Ultimately, Daniel provides hope and courage to people of any generation who strive to live faithful lives in "spiritual Babylon"—in cultures that demand the worship of many gods, not the One God; in the midst of temptation, trials, and persecution; in the shadow of hostile governments and rulers. In the words of King Darius, "The God of Daniel … is the living God, enduring forever; his kingdom shall not be destroyed, and his dominion shall be without end. He delivers and rescues, he works signs and wonders in heaven and on earth" (6:27).

B. Read the Story

Read **Daniel 1–7, 9, and 12** before you answer the questions. These chapters will give you the highlights of the book, focusing on the narrative portion. Next, locate the prophet Daniel on the *Timeline* Chart, paying attention to the time period and pertinent events of the time, to the rulers he served under, and to his location.

Going Deeper (optional): To get the entire story and message of this prophet, read the entire book of **Daniel.**

As always, pray before you read.

C. Take a Deeper Look

Answering these questions will draw you into the heart of the story. If you do not understand something, make a note of it to bring up in the small-group discussion.

Daniel in Nebuchadnezzar's Court (Daniel 1–6)

These chapters are full of empowering stories of faith in dire circumstances. Daniel and his companions represent the "faithful remnant" God nourished, protected, and guided during these seventy painful years of Babylonian exile.

1. Read **Daniel 1.** What kind of person is Daniel as a teenager?

2. Daniel and his companions are given new names, as noted in the following chart.

Hebrew Name	Meaning	Babylonian Name	Meaning
Daniel	"God is my judge"	Belteshazzar	"Bel protect the king!"
Hananiah	"Yahweh is gracious"	Shadrach	"Command of Aku [the moon god]"
Mishael	"Who is like God?"	Meshach	"Who is like Aku?"
Azariah	"Yahweh is a helper"	Abednego	"Servant of the shining one [Nego or Nebo]"

Read **CCC 203.** What is significant about the way these names are changed?

Who Are the Chaldeans?

Throughout these early chapters, Nebuchadnezzar consults magicians, enchanters, sorcerers, and Chaldeans.[4] These function like political consultants: They are well-educated, "wise men" who are trained in literature, writing, and administration, as well as in interpreting dreams and telling the future. They study the stars like modern-day pundits study economic tables and other signs of the times. By interpreting signs they read in the heavens, they aim to provide messages from the gods to guide the king.

3. Read **Daniel 2:1-23,** in which Nebuchadnezzar poses a seemingly impossible question: not only "interpret my dream," but also, "what did I dream?"

    a. Learning that he is slated to die along with the wise men who cannot tell the dream, Daniel seeks an audience with the king. What does Daniel intend to do, and how does he prepare?

    b. What does Daniel's prayer in verses 21-23 reveal about his knowledge of God?

4. Read **Daniel 2:24-49.**

    a. Nebuchadnezzar dreamed of a mighty and frightening image: a statue with a head of gold, breast and arms of silver, belly and thighs of bronze, legs of iron, and feet of iron and clay. What happens in his dream as he looks upon this image? (See **verses 34-35.**)

    b. What interpretation does God provide through Daniel to the king?

[4] "Chaldean," or "astrologer," as some Bibles translate it, is both a title and a nationality. Chaldea was a common name for Southern Mesopotamia. (You may recall that Abraham was called out of "Ur of the Chaldees.") The eleventh dynasty of the kings of Babylon, which began in 620 BC with Nabopolassar and ended with King Nabonidus and his son Belshazzar, is known as the Chaldean Dynasty. During that time, "Chaldean" was virtually synonymous with "Babylonian."

5. Read **Daniel 3.**[5] Perhaps inspired by his dream, King Nebuchadnezzar builds an enormous golden image, sixty by six cubits (ninety by nine feet) in size. He orders everyone in the kingdom to bow before it or be cast into a furnace of fire. Daniel's compatriots, themselves in positions of prominence in the kingdom, refuse.

   a. Read the king's question and the men's answer in verses 14-18. What is really at stake in this trial? (See the end of **verse 15.**)

   b. What happens to the men who refuse to bow to the image, and how do they respond to their punishment?

   c. How does Nebuchadnezzar respond?

6. The remnant of Judah has been exiled to the epicenter of worldly power and wisdom. The very fact of their exile seems to argue against the power of the LORD. Yet, when the LORD shows him the king's dream, Daniel says, "Blessed be the name of God forever and ever, for wisdom and power are his" (2:20). In the midst of a furnace, which might stand for the plight of Israel, Azariah and the others echo Daniel's praise in a powerful hymn.

   Read the Song in **verses 28-68** aloud (NAB: 3:52-90).[6]

   a. What three categories of beings are called upon to praise and glorify God? For help with this question, see sections beginning with **verses 36, 52, and 60** (NAB: 3:58, 74, 82).

[5] Text note: The section of Daniel 3 containing the prayers of Azariah and his companions was composed in Hebrew or Aramaic but then translated into Greek and preserved in the Septuagint. It appears in Catholic (but not Protestant) Bibles. Verse numbering varies with the translation. The RSV-CE numbers its verses from 1-68 and sets the prayers off in italics between 3:23 and 3:24. [They are named as "song verses" in this session to avoid confusion; see question 6a.] The NAB inserts the hymn directly into the text as verses 24-90 and re-numbers the remaining verses so they flow consecutively.

[6] Does the song sound familiar? This well-loved prayer is part of the prayers of the Divine Office, featured in Morning Prayer as an Old Testament Canticle.

7. Read **Daniel 6.** (Darius—"royal one"—is a Mede; he may have been a general appointed over Babylon, a governor with king-like powers.) What does Daniel's response to the king's decree show about the strength of his faith? (See **verse 10.**)

Daniel's Visions (Daniel 7–12)

Here, the genre changes from historical narrative to apocalyptic writing. Chapter 7 introduces the major themes of this section, which include the power of the state opposed to God; the ultimate victory of God over all powers; and the promised future deliverance of his people and the establishment of his kingdom. Like much apocalyptic literature, it features dramatic, often bizarre images that can be frightening and hard to understand. We will look at the broad strokes of the visions.

8. Read **Daniel 7,** in which Daniel receives a vision of God's view of the coming kingdoms, one that parallels the vision Nebuchadnezzar received in Chapter 2.

   a. Fill in the empty boxes below to show how Daniel sees the kingdoms that Nebuchadnezzar sees as parts of a human image.

World Empires[7]	**Nebuchadnezzar's Vision (Daniel 2:32-33) A statue of a man**	**Daniel's Vision (Daniel 7:3-7, 20) Four beasts**
1	Gold head	
2	Silver chest, arms	
3	Bronze belly, thighs	
4	Iron legs, Clay and iron feet	

   b. In Nebuchadnezzar's vision, a stone comes from nowhere and smashes the statue to nothing before growing to fill the earth. In Daniel's vision, God appears on a fiery throne and sits in judgment on the nations, destroying the last beast and taking away the dominion of the others. What does Daniel see next that corresponds to the stone in Daniel 2? (See **7:13-14.**)

[7] The visions propose a succession of world empires leading up to the establishment and spread of the kingdom of God. The traditional interpretation is that these world empires are Babylon, Medo-Persia, Greece, and Rome. Other scholars identify them as Babylon, Media, Persia, and Greece (however, the Medes were never an empire on their own).

The Stone and the Son of Man

The motif of the "stone" runs through the Old Testament and ends in our Lord Jesus Christ and his kingdom. For further study (optional), read the following Scripture passages and think about how they are connected.

Psalm 118:22	Isaiah 8:13-15	Isaiah 28:16
Matthew 21:42-44	Acts 4:11-12	1 Peter 2:6-8

Note that in Hebrew, there is even a "play" on the words "stone" *(eben)* and "son" *(ben).*

c. **New Testament Connection:** "Son of Man" is the title Jesus most often uses to refer to himself. Read the following verses and record what you learn about Jesus as Son of Man.

Matthew 25:31-32:

Matthew 24:30:

Matthew 17:12, 22-23:

In Matthew 16:13-23, Jesus calls himself "Son of Man." In doing so, he evokes Daniel's image of the Messiah coming in clouds of glory to judge the nations. At the same time, by announcing his passion, he gives that title a new meaning more in line with Isaiah's Suffering Servant: The Son of Man came not to be served but to serve and to give his life for those he came to save. True, his kingship will mean he is raised high to heaven—but it will come about first through Jesus being lifted on the Cross (see CCC 440).

In Chapter 9, Daniel—who is now an old man—realizes that the seventy-year period of exile prophesied by Jeremiah is coming to an end.[8] He goes before God in sackcloth and ashes, confessing the sins of the people and begging for forgiveness on their behalf. Read **Daniel 9:16-19.** For what does Daniel plead, and on what basis?

9. As Daniel continues in prayer, the angel Gabriel comes to enlighten him with "wisdom and understanding" of the future, because of God's great love for him (9:22-23). What, in general, does Gabriel tell him in 9:24?

10. Daniel is given further visions about the coming eras, in which the successive empires are the visible face of a battle in the heavens. In retrospect, we know that even after returning from exile, the Jews will live under a series of Gentile rulers for that 490-year period, which culminates at the time of Jesus Christ. Read **Daniel 12:1-3.** What hope is given to Daniel and, through him, to the people?

[8] See Jeremiah 25:11, 29:10-14.

Daniel Chapters 13–14

While most Protestant Bibles end with the vision of the resurrected in Daniel 12, the Catholic canon includes two additional chapters in Daniel. Only Greek manuscripts of these chapters have survived (which is likely why they are not included in the final Jewish canon, as the Jews by that time had forbidden even the learning of Greek). Daniel 13 and 14 were part of the Old Testament canon of the early Church (the Septuagint), and their inspiration was confirmed at the Council of Trent. Many scholars believe these chapters most likely were originally written in Aramaic or Hebrew.

Daniel 13 gives us the story of Susanna, whom Daniel defends from false testimony. In the narrative, he is a young man (Daniel 13:45), and in some manuscripts, this story is placed in its proper chronological order earlier in the Daniel narrative. Daniel 14 contains two additional stories: Bel (verses 1-22) and the dragon (verses 23-42). In each narrative, Daniel uses his God-given wisdom to expose Babylonian worship as a cleverly devised sham. The message? Only the God of Israel is worthy of worship and devotion.

D. Application

This question will help you apply one of the key themes of the session to your life. After meditating on it, respond to God with a brief written prayer if you choose.

Daniel and his companions stand out in the Old Testament as remarkable examples of faithful lives lived in the face of inconvenience, opposition, and persecution. A hymn called "Dare to Be a Daniel" used to be sung in their praise:

Standing by a purpose true,
Heeding God's command,
Honor them, the faithful few!
All hail to Daniel's band!

Refrain:

Dare to be a Daniel,
Dare to stand alone!
Dare to have a purpose firm!
Dare to make it known.

What inconveniences, opposition, or persecution do you face in your life that might prevent you from worshiping God? What have you learned from Daniel's life and visions that might help you "dare to be a Daniel"?

Dear Lord …

Session 8 Talk Notes

Daniel – Faithful to the End

I. Setting the Stage

A. Placement in Bible

B. Background

C. Spiritual wisdom for faithful living under fire

D. Babylon as a spiritual force

1. World powers, systems, structures opposed to God

    a. Genesis 11: Tower of Babel

    b. Revelation 18: the fall of Babylon

2. "The spirit of this world" (1 Corinthians 2:12)

    a. Seeks to displace God on the throne of our lives

    b. Aim to enslave humanity with false freedoms

3. Two strategies, physical and spiritual

E. Book of Daniel

1. Messages of hope

2. Structure

    a. Central apocalyptic visions (Chapters 7–12)

        i. The future fate of world powers

        ii. "Apocalyptic" = "unveiling"

    b. Two narrative "bookends" (Chapters 1–6, 13–14)

    c. Message: ultimate triumph of righteousness

II. The Strategies of Babylon (Physical and Spiritual)

A. Remove the wealth (sacred vessels, human treasure)

1. Daniel, Hananiah, Azariah, Mishael (1:6)

2. Exiled more than nine hundred miles from home
3. Spiritual Babylon follows same strategy

B. Seduce with rich food and wine (1:5-16)

1. An appeal to the passions
2. Eating would defile them
   a. Not kosher
   b. Meat sacrificed to idols
   c. Meals imply fellowship
   d. Parallel in New Testament Corinth
3. Daniel "resolved not to defile himself" (verse 8)
   a. A pre-determined attitude
   b. Hebrew: He purposed in his heart, set it "like a pillar in the ground"
4. Daniel's courage inspired his friends
   a. 2 Maccabees 7:7-42 – young men refuse food of Greeks
   b. Mother encourages to trust (language of resurrection)
5. Lessons for us
   a. Decide in advance
   b. Faithfulness in little things – build life of virtue
   c. Gandalf in *The Hobbit:* importance of everyday deeds
6. Daniel and friends blessed for their faithfulness

C. Give them new names, change identity (verses 6-7)

1. Their Hebrew names are theophoric, recall God's character
2. The new names brand them as servants of Babylon
3. Daniel, friends do not allow new names to change hearts

III. Narratives Demonstrate Faithfulness

A. The fiery furnace (Daniel 3)[9]

1. Nebuchadnezzar demands worship of himself
2. The young men refuse (verses 16-18) and are thrown into fire
3. They praise the LORD in the midst of the fire (3:23ff)
    a. An appeal to God's mercy (verses 11-12)
    b. Verses 67-68 litany: "His mercy endures forever"
        i. Liturgy of the Hours, Sunday morning canticle
4. Nebuchadnezzar sees one "like the son of God" with them (3:92)
    a. Aramaic *bar elahin,* literally, "the son of God"
    b. Compare Matthew 18:20
    c. Praise as a sign to the world of God's power
5. The fruit of their faithfulness
    a. Nebuchadnezzar honors God publicly
    b. The young men are freed and honored

B. Daniel and the lion's den (Chapter 6)

1. Seventy years later; Daniel is old, highly regarded
2. Jealous enemies plot to destroy him
3. Daniel continues habits of worship, the source of his strength
4. Result: Daniel vindicated, King Darius praises God
5. A powerful witness to Maccabees, later Christians

IV. The Importance of Perseverance in Faith, Even Under Fire

V. Conclusion: Prayer of Renewal[10]

---

[9] Note discrepancies in verse numbering among translations of Daniel (see footnote on page 74).

[10] For the text of this prayer, which is prayed at the close of each session, see page 12.

Prophets of the Return (538–167 BC)
Introduction to Session 9

Who would have believed that after less than a century of dominance over the Middle East, the powerful Babylonian Empire would be swallowed up by the Persians? (See the Persian Empire map on page 10.) This new world power, centered in what is today Iran, will shape the destiny of the Jewish people from 539 BC until the arrival of Alexander the Great two hundred years later (333 BC).

With the miraculous decree of Cyrus (Ezra 1:2-4), which had been foretold in Isaiah 44:28–45:1, the Jews return to their burned and broken land to begin the process of rebuilding the Temple and Jerusalem's protective walls. Many of the people move back to Judea in three "waves" of return from exile.

First Return 538 BC	Ezra 1:1–2:2	Cyrus' decree to return and rebuild the Temple. A large group of exiles returns, led by Zerubbabel.
Second Return 458 BC	Ezra 7	The priest Ezra is sent by Artaxerxes; he reinstates proper worship and teaches the Law.
Third Return 444 BC	Nehemiah 1–2	Nehemiah returns and rebuilds the Jerusalem walls.

Take a moment to look at the yellow "Return" period on your *Bible Timeline* Chart where those three returns are pictured as three yellow arrows. Notice the key events on the Chart and the people involved. These events form the backdrop for the prophets we are about to study.

God sends prophets to speak to those who have returned to the Promised Land to bring them hope. These prophets are Haggai, Zechariah, and Malachi. Find their names on the Chart. In Session 9, we will get to know them before we move on to take a look at "New Testament and Modern Prophets" in our final session.

Session 9 – Questions

Haggai and Malachi – Messengers of Hope

A. Establish the Context

Perhaps the most important building project during the challenging decades of Judah's return home from exile involves not a stone structure but the people of God themselves. They have returned home, but the reality of their situation does not match up with the glorious promise of restoration. For one thing, the land they return to is not "theirs." What once was Israel and Judah remains a province of Persia, with local authorities under the control of the Persian king. The promised restoration under a Davidic king has not begun. Understanding and living in this "already but not yet" state of affairs is a challenge as they must continue to live by faith, waiting.

Three prophets give voice to God's Word during this post-exilic time period. We will look at two of them in this session: **Haggai** and **Malachi.** The tiny book of Haggai provides our first window into the Return. Seventeen years after returning from exile, this prophet paints an anything-but-rosy picture of the situation. Poor harvests, misplaced priorities, lackluster devotion, and poor morale have led to a kind of spiritual paralysis. Haggai (with his partner prophet, Zechariah) "builds up" the people of God as they work to complete the long-stalled Temple building project. Haggai and Malachi are prophets of hope who encourage their contemporaries even as they point to something in the future that will be greater than the physical Temple—a full and glorious restoration of the Davidic throne and a messianic age to come.

Our second window into the Return is Malachi, whose book completes the Old Testament prophetic age. Nearly a century after Zechariah and Haggai (c. 433 BC), Malachi battles priest scandals, rampant divorce, religious indifference, day-labor wage controversies, and oppression of the poor. Does this sound familiar? Though he lived nearly 2,500 years ago, his message remains contemporary and convicting. The text is shaped around a series of disputes between the people and God. Like his predecessors, Malachi closes with a promise of Elijah's return and a powerful image of the LORD, pictured as the "sun of righteousness" returning to his earthly Temple (see Malachi 4:2, 5). Malachi's emphasis on the constant, undergirding love of God forms a fitting close to the Book of the Twelve, which opened with God's call of love through Hosea.

B. Read the Story

Read **Haggai** and **Malachi** before you answer the questions (both books are very short). Along with Zechariah, they can be found in the RSV-CE right before 1 and 2 Maccabees, which bring the Old Testament to a close.[1] In the NAB and New Jerusalem versions, they can be found at the end of the Old Testament.

Make sure you can locate Haggai and Malachi in the Return (yellow) portion of the *Timeline* Chart, paying attention to the historical context and pertinent events.

Going Deeper (optional): To get the entire story and message of these prophets, read the historical background found in **Ezra 1–7** (for Haggai) and in the entire book of **Nehemiah** (for Malachi).

As always, pray before you read.

---

1 1 and 2 Maccabees follow Esther in the NAB.

C. Take a Deeper Look

Answering these questions will draw you into the heart of the story. If you do not understand something, make a note of it to bring up in the small-group discussion.

HAGGAI

Historical Background from the Book of Ezra

1. All three prophets of the Return should be read in the context of the historical background conveyed in the books of Ezra and Nehemiah. Ezra 1–6 tells of the first return (under Zerubbabel) and of the building of the Temple.

   a. Read **Ezra 1:1–2:2.** How does God bring about an end to the time of Babylonian exile?

   b. The people do not return to an empty land. Judea is now a province of Persia, administered from Samaria and populated by the unskilled, uneducated people the Babylonians have left behind. In the countryside to the north are the descendants of exiles from other lands (moved there by the Assyrians). These have mixed Israelite practices with the worship of other gods.[2] Read **Ezra 4.** Briefly describe how the returned exiles fare as they work to build the Temple.

The Word of the Lord Comes by Haggai (Book of Haggai)

Sixteen years after construction is stopped, Haggai comes on the scene. His little book covers the final months of 520 BC during the second year of the reign of the Persian king Darius I. Addressed to the Judean governor, Zerubbabel, and to the high priest Joshua, the message comprises a series of four "words" from the Lord.

2. Read **Haggai 1,** which describes the first "word" or message from God.

   a. The Temple has lain in ruins for decades. What have the people been doing? Where have they placed their priorities?

   b. Has focusing on their own priorities paid off for them? Explain (see **verses 5-6 and 9-11**).

2 See 2 Kings 17:24-41.

3. a. Although they are back in the land, blessings do not automatically follow. Read about the covenant promises and curses God gives them through Moses in **Deuteronomy 28:1-6 and 15-19.** What do you learn?

   b. What is the solution to their struggle? (See also **Haggai 1:8.**)

4. Given the determined opposition the people face, one might be tempted to excuse them for letting the Temple go until a more opportune time. Read **1 Kings 6:11-13 and 8:41-43.** Why is it so important for the LORD to have a "house" in the world?

5. Review **Haggai 1:12-14.** When Zerubbabel, Joshua, and the people respond in obedience, what message and concrete help does God give them? (See also **2:4-5.**)

6. Ezra 3:10-12 describes how those who are old enough to remember the original Temple weep at the sight of the new foundation. Solomon had vast resources at his disposal, and the original Temple was glorious. It is obvious, even at this early stage of building, that the new structure is no match for the first. According to **Haggai 2:4-9,** should they be concerned? Why, or why not?

7. The theme of "considering" runs through Haggai. In just two chapters, the people are asked three times to consider how they have fared as they have pursued their own priorities to no avail—because they have failed to return to God (1:5, 7, 2:15, 18). Read those verses and **Haggai 2:18-20.** What encouraging thing should they "consider from this day onward"?

The Third Prophet of the Return: Zechariah

Zechariah, who we will not have time to study, enters the picture at the same time as Haggai. His name means "Yahweh remembers," and he bears a message of hope: God has not forgotten his people, however it may seem. He has a plan. The promised restoration is on the way. Through Zechariah, God calls his people: "Return to me, says the LORD of hosts, and I will return to you" (Zechariah 1:3).

Zechariah speaks not only of the Temple that is being restored, but also of a glorious Temple of the future. In a series of dramatic visions, he looks through the current situation to reveal what the temporal realities represent, a true and final restoration: not only a new Temple, but a New Jerusalem that will abide in peace; the day of the LORD and the end of the opposing nations; a restored priesthood; and the coming messianic Servant, the future Davidic king, who will remove sin from their midst.

"Sing and rejoice, O daughter of Zion; for lo, I come and I will dwell in the midst of you, says the LORD. And many nations shall join themselves to the LORD in that day, and shall be my people; and I will dwell in the midst of you, and you shall know that the LORD of hosts has sent me to you. And the LORD will inherit Judah as his portion in the holy land, and will again choose Jerusalem" (2:10-12).

Despite these hope-filled words, the question lingers long after Zechariah: When will this "day" be, and when will the LORD return to his Temple? For even though the Temple is built and the people respond to God's call, Scripture never records the filling of this rebuilt Temple with the Spirit of God's presence. All will remain in a state of "already, but not yet" waiting until one day when a young woman will take her child, Emmanuel—"God with us"—to be presented there.

Not surprisingly, Zechariah's prophecies figure heavily in the Gospel accounts of the final week of Jesus' life, the time we call Holy Week. From Zechariah, for example, comes the prophecy that Jerusalem's King comes "humble and riding on an ass, on a colt the foal of an ass" (9:9). Some of the imagery in Revelation is drawn from his visions, along with those of Isaiah, Daniel, and Ezekiel. See the chart on pages 15-16 for some of the images from Zechariah and other prophets that are taken up by the Gospel writers to demonstrate that Jesus is the Messiah.

MALACHI

Historical Background from the Books of Ezra and Nehemiah

The second half of Ezra picks up in 458 BC (years after the building of the Temple) when Ezra himself goes to Jerusalem. Sent by King Artaxerxes to check on things and to take with him provisions for the Temple, Ezra is accompanied by nearly two thousand returning exiles. He is a priest and a scribe, "skilled in the law of Moses" (Ezra 7:6), and he instructs the people in the Law and brings about reform. Then in 445 BC, there is a third return: Nehemiah, cupbearer to the king, is distressed by reports of the broken, fire-ravaged state of the walls of Jerusalem. He asks Artaxerxes to send him to rebuild the walls of Jerusalem. He returns, and under his leadership, the wall is rebuilt in fifty-two days in spite of severe opposition from their neighbors (Nehemiah 4:7-9).

8. Read **Nehemiah 13:4-31,** which describes the state of Judea when Nehemiah returns after an absence. Describe briefly the four things Nehemiah finds that trouble him.

The Word of the Lord Comes by Malachi (Book of Malachi)

Around 433 BC, toward the end of Nehemiah's term as governor and before a series of reforms enacted by Ezra and Nehemiah, the Word of the Lord comes to the people through a prophet called Malachi (in Hebrew, "my messenger"). In a series of six disputations, Malachi calls the people back to covenant faithfulness to a God who has always loved them and who offers the future hope of a glorious day of the Lord.

9. "I have loved you," says the Lord in Malachi 1:2. Yet the people do not see it. They are blinded by their own sins. Read the following verses and note the ways the covenant is broken.

Malachi	Covenant Broken	Breaches of the Covenant
2:1-9	The covenant of Levi, "a covenant of life and peace" (verse 5)	
2:10-11	"The covenant of our fathers" (verse 10)	
2:14-16	The covenant of marriage ("between you and the wife of your youth," verse 14)	

10. In **Malachi 2:17,** we read that the people protest this characterization of themselves. They wonder how it can matter whether they follow the Law, when it seems as though lawbreakers get away with wrong and are blessed by the Lord.

    a. To those who believe God does not act when his Law is broken, Malachi announces in 3:2 "the day of his coming" in judgment, but asks, "who can endure" that day? Read the following passages and tell what that day will bring.

Malachi 3:1-5:

Malachi 4:1:

b. In light of God's coming in fiery judgment on that day, is there hope for anyone? Read **Malachi 3:6-7,** and record what you learn.

11. Malachi 3 and 4 speak of someone who will come just prior to the day of the LORD. What do the following verses tell you about this person and his purpose?

Verses in Malachi	Person and Description	Purpose
3:1		
4:5-6 (NAB or New Jerusalem: 3:23-24)		

12. Now read **Malachi 4:1-6** (NAB and New Jerusalem: Malachi 3:19-24).

a. While "all the arrogant and all evildoers" will be as though burned to stubble at the day of the LORD, what can be expected by those who fear the LORD?

b. Compare **verses 5-6** (NAB: 3:23-24) with **Luke 1:17,** which is part of the angel Gabriel's message to Zechariah. (For context, read **Luke 1:8-17.**) What interpretation does the angel give to Malachi's prophecy?

13. Read **James 4:6-9.** What does this add to your understanding of God's love and judgment and how we can approach him, even now?

D. Application

This question will help you apply one of the key themes of the session to your life. After meditating on it, respond to God with a brief written prayer if you choose.

In our time, Pope Francis has renewed the call from Jesus, originally heard by St. Francis of Assisi, to "rebuild my Church." What spiritual building projects does the Church face today? What are the challenges? How are you participating?

Dear Lord …

Session 9 Talk Notes

Haggai and Malachi – Messengers of Hope

I. Setting the Stage

A. Background of the Return

1. Three "waves" of return

2. Exiles return to three building projects

a. Rebuild the Temple (Zerubbabel 538 BC)

b. Rebuild the people (Ezra)

c. Rebuild the walls of Jerusalem (Nehemiah)

3. Opposition

a. Interior (personal sin, laziness)

b. From without (Samaritans)

i. *Shatan* (Satan): "adversary, accuser"

B. God's messengers of hope: Zechariah, Haggai, Malachi

II. Haggai

A. With Zechariah, God's messenger at start of Return

B. 520 BC, fifteen years after work stopped on second Temple

C. Ezra 5:2: Prophets help rebuild

1. Hebrew, *seh-ad'* (to sustain, support, encourage, strengthen, refresh)

a. Used to God helping us

b. Psalm 94:18 – If my foot slips, God's loving kindness will hold me up *(seh-ad')*

2. God sends prophets to hold them up, encourage

D. God's message: They are building their own homes instead of God's house

1. "Consider how you have fared" (three times)

a. Literally, "Apply your hearts to your paths"

b. Notice lack of blessing, result of covenant unfaithfulness

2. Be faithful and I will bless

a. Matthew 6:33 – Seek first the kingdom, and all shall be added

b. Matthew 6:21 – Where your treasure is, your heart will be

E. The people obey and the LORD is with them (1:12-13)

1. Experience of his presence follows faithful obedience

2. The LORD helps them overcome acedia (spiritual apathy)

a. The LORD "stirred up the spirit" of leaders and people (1:14)

b. They came back and built God's house

3. Pattern: God prompts, we respond in faith, he supplies the strength

F. The people face discouragement

1. The Temple falls short of the glory of the original

2. God meets them where they are, gives hope (2:4-5)

a. Be strong, I am with you

b. Your past efforts led to nothing, but from now on I will bless you

c. Their preparations will prepare the "house" for a King coming in glory

III. Zechariah

A. Series of visions, single message

1. God working out his purpose

2. Apocalyptic imagery

B. Points to future fulfillment of what the Temple symbolizes

IV. Malachi

A. Background

1. Sixty years later, another wave of exiles return under Ezra

2. Zerubbabel returns but no king; rebuilding, but promises seem forgotten

3. Malachi the last of the Old Testament prophets, c. 430 BC

4. Malachi means "my messenger"

5. Message prepares for Messiah during time of waiting, speaks to us

B. Structure: series of six dialogues

C. Problems addressed

1. Types of problems apply to us as well

2. People doubt God's love and faithfulness (Chapter 1)

a. God's love in spite of appearances

b. God is almighty

c. God is faithful

i. Can they be faithful during time of waiting?

ii. Can they return his love in true worship, obedience?

d. They are not faithful to God or his covenant

i. Reflected in unfaithfulness to marriage covenant

ii. "I hate divorce" (2:15-16)

iii. Marriage: a sign of God's covenant love

iv. Divorce: a "countersign" of unfaithfulness

3. Why should we serve God when the evil prosper?

a. Judgment is coming to reward good, punish evil

b. God will come with purifying fire (3:1-3)

i. Fiery language continued in 4:1-3

ii. In the meantime, remember the law (4:4)

c. God sending Elijah before the future "Day of the LORD"

i. Quoted in reference to John the Baptist (Luke 1:17)

ii. He will turn the hearts of fathers and children to each other (4:6)

iii. Preparing the way for a New Covenant family of God

iv. "Return to me and I will return to you" (3:7)

4. The "Return" is just a beginning

V. Conclusion: Prayer of Renewal[3]

[3] For the text of this prayer, which is prayed at the close of each session, see page 12.

New Testament and Modern Prophets
Introduction to Session 10

Before we continue beyond the Old Testament era, it will be helpful to briefly recall some of the prophetic messages we have heard.

Hosea: The marriage-like covenant between God and Israel has been violated by the Northern Kingdom of Israel, and that nation is being "destroyed for lack of knowledge" (4:6) of God. Hosea lives out his message, marrying a prostitute to show how God's merciful love is more powerful than any sin. God promises "tough love" should his people not return: judgment with the ultimate aim of restoring them to blessing in an intimate relationship with him.

Jonah: Jonah's life proclaims a startling message to an Israel that feels it has a corner on God's favor: God has merciful compassion on everyone who turns to him, whether Jew or Gentile. Even the wicked Assyria is shown mercy; because the people repent, they are saved for a time.

Isaiah 1–39: Sometimes called the "Book of Woe," the first half of the book of Isaiah is full of warning. The Southern Kingdom of Judah may be ruled by David's heirs and may house the holy Temple, but it has lost the bloom of its first love. It has become sinful and corrupt and is in danger of turning to other gods. In the days of the Assyrian threat leading up to the fall of the Northern Kingdom, Isaiah calls the people to repentance and warns of impending exile for the south as well. The land will be destroyed along with the earthly throne—but God will remain faithful. A remnant will be saved, and a child who will be born to a virgin will restore and establish God's kingdom.

Isaiah 40–66: Often called the "Book of Consolation," the second half of the book of Isaiah peers into the future and proclaims a message of comfort set during the time of Babylonian Exile and beyond. The situation will seem bleak. But punishment, even though deserved, is for but a time and is meant to restore. Through Isaiah, God promises the restoration of the nation (even naming Cyrus as agent of their return) and bids them look forward to a glorious future kingdom when all will be healed. Part and parcel of that is the coming of God's "Servant" who will bring justice, speak God's Word, and bear the people's sins: not only those of Israel, but those of the world.

Jeremiah: For four decades leading up to the destruction of Jerusalem, Jeremiah is a prophet of both doom and restoration. God has been patient, but the time for judgment has come. The existence of the Temple does not protect them from enemies. Jeremiah announces judgment to people who have forsaken God and do not want to listen—all the while proclaiming God's merciful plan to restore them.

Ezekiel: Exiled to Babylon, Ezekiel brings a vision of God's continued presence with his people. He is a "watchman on the wall," warning them of Jerusalem's destruction and promising a new, everlasting covenant in which they will be raised as from death and replanted in Israel to be shepherded by God himself and his Anointed One (the Messiah). This has the "already but not yet" nature of an initial, physical return to the land followed by a future, "internal" return when new hearts and spirits will enable them to walk in obedient love.

Daniel speaks prophetically of the future even as he models the way to live a faithful life under foreign domination. In spite of appearances, God has a plan, and everything is under his control. Ultimately all kingdoms will fall before the just and righteous kingdom of God, whose universal reign will last forever.

Haggai reprimands the returned exiles for neglecting their task of rebuilding the Temple and focusing on rebuilding their own homes instead. They are not being blessed, because even though they have returned to the land, they remain spiritually far from God. He exhorts them to take courage and work to build God's house, and then they will be blessed.

Malachi assures a people who have broken God's covenant in many ways that God loves them and is coming to refine the priests and to judge those who oppose him. The same fire that burns the proud and evildoers will heal and restore those who fear (revere) him. They should walk in obedience and wait patiently for the LORD's messenger, Elijah, who will prepare the people for his coming.

Did Prophecy End with the Old Testament?

In our final session, we will consider ways in which Jesus fulfills the prophetic expectations of the Old Testament as the ultimate, promised Prophet, and we will see how the prophetic witness continues in the Church.

Session 10 – Questions

New Testament and Modern Prophets – Messengers of the New Covenant

In many and various ways God spoke of old to our fathers by the prophets; but in these last days he has spoken to us by a Son. … He reflects the glory of God and bears the very stamp of his nature, upholding the universe by his word of power.

– Hebrews 1:1, 3

A. Establish the Context

The messages of Haggai, Zechariah, and Malachi brought us to the end of the Old Testament prophets in Session 9. Each of the faithful messengers of God we have studied was called to speak a word from the Lord into his time and place: a word that assured Israel of God's love and called them back into a personal relationship with the Father, lived out in faithfulness to the divine covenant. Through the prophets, God maintained a dialog with his people even when they were not listening. Through them, God's voice resounded in three critical periods of Israel's history: the time of the Divided Kingdom; the years of Babylonian Exile; and the long, difficult time of Return to the land.

Several more centuries elapse until the time "before Christ" (i.e., BC) comes to a close. It is a time that requires patient waiting for the appearance of Elijah and the day of the Lord; it is a time of incubation of sorts until the hour is ripe for the Messiah's coming. No new prophetic word is given during that time, and a word of the Lord spoken a thousand years before still hangs in the air: "I will raise up for them a prophet like [Moses] from among their brethren; and I will put my words in his mouth, and he shall speak to them all that I command him" (Deuteronomy 18:18). No one could have imagined that this promised Prophet, Isaiah's Servant, the Shepherd, and the Messiah would come together all at once, wrapped in a bundle of swaddling clothes and laid in a Bethlehem manger. Nor could they imagine that not only would this prophet speak the Word of God, he would *be* the Word of God, definitively proclaiming and embodying all that this Word means.

As foretold by Malachi, John the Baptist bursts onto the scene "in the fullness of time," filled with the spirit and power of Elijah, preparing the way for the "sun of righteousness" as he comes "with healing in his wings" (see Malachi 4). This final session in our study begins here, with the One who is announced. Who is he, and how does he fulfill all that the prophets foretold? And once that definitive Word of God speaks with his life: What happens to the prophetic office? We will take a look at other New Testament prophets and at the sense in which the prophetic office continues even now in the Church.

B. Read the Story

There is no advance reading for this session. Read the particular Scripture passages as they are brought up in the questions.

C. Take a Deeper Look

Answering these questions will draw you into the heart of the story. If you do not understand something, make a note of it to bring up in the small-group discussion.

The Long-Expected Prophet Comes

1. John the Baptist fulfills the prophecy in Isaiah 40 of one who will come to prepare the way of the Lord. Read **Luke 3:1-18.**

   a. What does John do to prepare the way for Jesus?

   b. How is his message like that of the Old Testament prophets?

2. If John the Baptist is the messenger or forerunner announced by Malachi, Jesus is the One whose coming he announces.[1] Matthew purposefully draws attention to events in Jesus' life that fulfill messianic prophecies. Choose four or more of the following passages and tell how Jesus fulfills the prophecies that are quoted in them. The Old Testament references are provided for your information.

   Matthew 1:18-23 (Isaiah 7:14 and 8:8, 10):

   Matthew 2:1-6 (Micah 5:2):

   Matthew 2:13-15 (Hosea 11:1):

   Matthew 4:12-16 (Isaiah 9:1-2, 42:7; Amos 5:8):

   Matthew 8:14-17 (Isaiah 53:4):

---

1 See Matthew 3:11-12; Mark 1:1-11; Luke 3:1-22; John 1:19-34.

Matthew 13:34-35 (Psalm 78:2):[2]

Matthew 21:1-5 (Zechariah 9:9):

3. Not only does Jesus fulfill messianic prophecy, he also is the "ultimate" prophet.

   a. Read **Deuteronomy 18:15, 18-19,** and describe what was promised more than one thousand years before the birth of Christ.

   b. Read the following verses and comment on who recognizes Jesus as that prophet, and why. (You may want to start a few verses ahead of each passage to get the context.)

      John 6:14:

      Acts 3:20-26:

      John 8:26, 28:

4. Now read **Hebrews 1:1-3 and 2:1-3.** In what way is Jesus a prophet in an even deeper sense than the Old Testament prophets were?

5. The renowned Jewish scholar Abraham Heschel wrote that the prophet is "one who bears testimony to God's concern for human beings. … His fundamental objective was to reconcile man and God."[3] **Think About It:** How does Jesus exemplify this in a most perfect manner? (For help with this question, read **John 3:16** and **Colossians 1:19-20.**)

---

2 Psalm 78 is attributed to Asaph, who is called a prophet in 2 Chronicles 29:30 (LXX).

3 Abraham J. Heschel, *The Prophets* (New York: HarperCollins, 1962), xviii, xxix.

The Prophetic Witness Continues in the New Testament

6. The Word of God is so completely spoken in Jesus that it is hard to imagine a need for prophets after him. Yet, that Word of God must continue to be shared with those who have not heard. Read Jesus' words to the apostles in **Acts 1:8,** just before his ascension. What does he say, and how might his words be seen as a continuation of what we have seen in the prophets of the Old Testament?

7. **Reviewing the Context:** In Jeremiah 31, we see that God promises to make a New Covenant with his people in which his law will be written on their hearts and minds so they can know him. It is not clear how this will happen. A clue comes in Ezekiel 37, where we see his vision of the dry bones springing to life under the power of the Spirit of God. The prophet Joel (who we do not study in this program) makes a similar prophecy regarding the Spirit that will come about "in those days and at that time" (Joel 3:1; NAB: Joel 4:1).

   a. Read **Joel 2:28-29** (NAB: 3:1-2). According to this, what will be the result of this awaited outpouring of the Spirit, and on whom will it fall?

   b. Now read **Acts 2:1-18.** What happens in the early days after Christ's resurrection and ascension that shows this time has come?

8. **Think About It:** Note how the following passages reflect the continuation of the prophetic witness in the early days of the Church.

   Acts 8:25:

   Acts 8:34-35:

Acts 15:22-27:

9. In addition to the type of prophetic witness described above, St. Paul speaks of a "spiritual gift" of prophecy that is given to some.

   a. Read **1 Corinthians 14:1-4.** What does Paul say about prophecy's desirability and function in the Church?

   b. Note some of the ways in which the gift of prophecy is manifested.

   Acts 11:27-28:

   Acts 15:32:

   c. Read **CCC 799–801.** What else do you learn about charisms there?

Prophetic Witness in the Church Today

10. We have seen how the Old Testament prophets foreshadow the ultimate Prophet, Jesus Christ, who has been made "priest, prophet, and king" by God. Every Christian participates by virtue of baptism in these three offices.[4] According to CCC 905, what is one way lay people fulfill their prophetic mission?

[4] See CCC 783, 904.

11. The Church has given us beautiful guidance as we seek to live our share of Christ's prophetic office. Consider the following paragraphs from *Lumen Gentium,* the Second Vatican Council's document on the Church.

    "The holy people of God shares also in Christ's prophetic office; it spreads abroad a living witness to him, especially by means of a life of faith and charity and by offering to God a sacrifice of praise, the tribute of lips which give praise to his name.[5] …

    "Christ, the great Prophet, who proclaimed the Kingdom of his Father both by the testimony of his life and the power of his words, continually fulfills his prophetic office until the complete manifestation of glory. He does this not only through the hierarchy who teach in his name and with his authority, but also through the laity whom he made his witnesses and to whom he gave understanding of the faith *(sensus fidei)* and an attractiveness in speech[6] so that the power of the Gospel might shine forth in their daily social and family life. They conduct themselves as children of the promise, and thus strong in faith and in hope they make the most of the present,[7] and with patience await the glory that is to come.[8] Let them not, then, hide this hope in the depths of their hearts, but even in the program of their secular life let them express it by a continual conversion and by wrestling 'against the world-rulers of this darkness, against the spiritual forces of wickedness.'"[9]

    In what specific ways can we spread his witness? List three ways that stand out to you from these paragraphs in *Lumen Gentium.*

D. Application

This question will help you apply one of the key themes of the session to your life. After meditating on it, respond to God with a brief written prayer if you choose.

Read the paragraphs from *Lumen Gentium* in question 11 again. Ask the Lord to show you one area in which you could improve your own witness to faith in him. What is it? Think of one thing you can do this week to better live out your prophetic calling, and commit to doing it. If you are afraid or reluctant: What have you learned from your study of the Old Testament prophets that provides courage or strength?

Dear Lord …

5 *Lumen Gentium* 12; see Hebrews 13:15.

6 See Acts 2:17-18; Revelation 19:10.

7 See Ephesians 5:16; Colossians 4:5.

8 See Romans 8:25.

9 *Lumen Gentium* 35, quoting Ephesians 6:12.

Session 10 Talk Notes

New Testament and Modern Prophets – Messengers of the New Covenant

I. Setting the Stage

A. John the Baptist
  1. "More than a prophet" (CCC 719)
  2. Completes cycle of prophets begun by Elijah

B. The prophetic mission and message continue
  1. Jesus Christ, the ultimate prophet
     a. Hebrews 1:1
  2. Prophets in the New Testament

C. Prophets today: God speaks through the Church
  1. CCC 79
  2. Teaching office addresses signs of the times (example: *Humanae Vitae*)

II. Our Participation in the Prophetic Nature of the Church

A. You were chosen by God
  1. Ephesians 1:4 – "before the foundation of the world"
  2. Anointed at baptism
  3. Affirmed: "Amen"

B. Distinction between rare charism of prophecy and universal prophetic character of the baptized
  1. Charism: speaking prophetic words
     a. Requires spiritual maturity, discernment
     b. Must be submitted to the Church, measured against divine revelation
     c. 1 Thessalonians 5:21 – "test everything; hold fast what is good"
  2. Private revelation discerned by the Church
     a. CCC 67

C. Our message
  1. Content: the gospel
  2. Proclamation = "evangelization"

D. The "New Evangelization"
  1. Same message but new ardor, methods, expressions
  2. Need to accept and walk in our baptismal anointing
  3. Be faithful where you are

III. How to Share the Good News

A. Know the story of salvation

B. Know the gospel message

1. Love, mercy, forgiveness; God inviting us into relationship
2. The kingdom is at hand
    a. God created us for life with him, a life of goodness and meaning that begins now and lasts forever

    b. Jesus is the face of the kingdom

    c. The Cross reveals God's love

    d. Resurrection: We walk in his risen life

C. Share *your* story

1. If God is part of your story, this is important
2. What has your spiritual journey up until now been like?
3. Write your testimony in one hundred words
    a. 1 Peter 3:15 – Be ready!
4. The importance of personal witness
    a. Benedict XVI on St. Paul

    b. "Modern man listens more willingly to witnesses than to teachers" (Paul VI)[10]

    c. When faith is lived out in your life, content makes sense

D. Importance of joy

1. The inner delight of knowing we are deeply loved by God
2. "Joy is a net of love by which you can catch souls" (Blessed Teresa of Calcutta)
3. Peter Kreeft: Lack of joy in Christians is cited by some as evidence against God's existence
4. In spiritual opposition
    a. Be not afraid

    b. God equips those he calls

IV. A Prophet Also Comforts the Afflicted

A. St. Paul on prophets (1 Corinthians 14:1-3)

1. Upbuilding, encouragement, consolation
2. Example: Barnabas ("son of encouragement") in Paul, Mark

B. The prophetic message of mercy

1. Jesus' message (Luke 4:18-19)
2. Aristides to Emperor Hadrian: the remarkable love of early Christians[11]

V. Conclusion: Prayer of Renewal[12]

---

10 *Evangelii Nuntiandi* 41.

11 *Apology of Aristides*, XV.

12 For the text of this prayer, which is prayed at the close of each session, see page 12.

Responses to the Study Questions

How to Use These Responses

After completing the home preparation, discussing the questions, and viewing the video presentation, the final step is to review the responses to the questions. These responses summarize the main points from the session and help you continue your Bible study in the next session.

Although it can be tempting to read these responses ahead of time, please wait until after you have completed the questions for each session and engaged in the small-group discussion. It is not necessary to have the "right" answers before going to the small-group discussion. In fact, one purpose of the discussion is for participants to learn by sharing their insights and questions with each other and, through that discussion, coming to a better understanding of the Scripture passages. This makes for a better Bible study experience for everyone.

For best results, follow these steps in order:

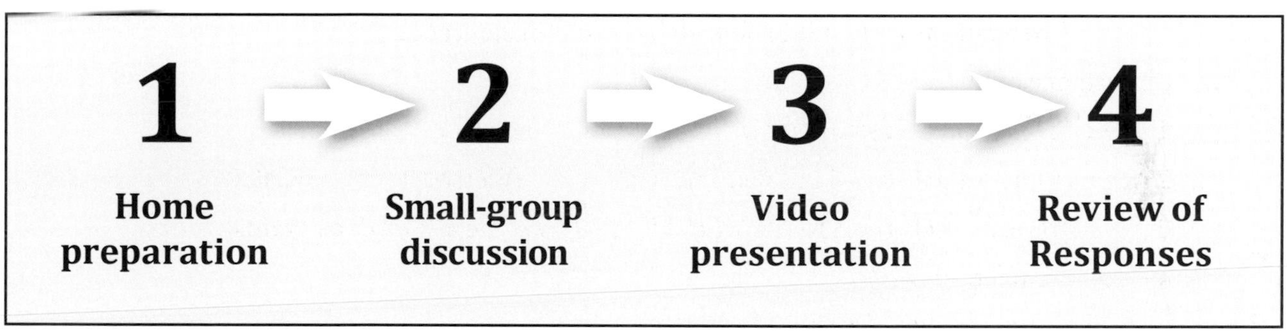

There are no responses for Session 1.

Session 2 – Responses

Hosea – Living God's Love Story

Facilitators: *Read these recommended responses to the questions ahead of time to help you prepare to lead the small-group discussion.*

Participants: *Reinforce what you have learned by reviewing these recommended responses after the small-group discussion and before you continue to the next session.*

A. Establish the Context

Facilitators: Take a moment to establish the context and what was learned in the previous session.

B. Read the Story

Facilitators: If there is time, have someone read each passage aloud before it is discussed.

C. Take a Deeper Look

Hosea's Marriage and Children (Hosea 1–3)

1. *The first chapter of Hosea gives us a snapshot of the entire book. Carefully re-read* ***Hosea 1:1–2:1.***

   a. *If a prophet is one who speaks for God and reveals his heart, Hosea certainly does so in a unique and painful way. Explain how Hosea dramatically reveals God's heart to Israel.*

   Hosea's relationship with the unfaithful Gomer reflects the relationship God has with Israel in a very real and painful way. God has joined himself to Israel in a "marriage" covenant, only to be jilted as she runs after other gods and ceases to love him. Hosea enters into that experience by living it out—he marries "a wife of harlotry"[1] (1:2) who bears three children named in ways that reflect the consequences of Israel's infidelity to God.

   b. *Hosea and Gomer have three children. Each name is a message, and as the years pass, the messages grow in seriousness. What is the meaning of each name? (Note: Some Bible versions provide only the English translations of the original Hebrew names. The list below is in order of appearance in the text.)*

   Jezreel:[2] Naming a child after the valley where Jeroboam's predecessor Jehu slaughtered the royal family and usurped the throne of Israel is a reminder of the way Jehu's family has come to power and a prediction that they will fall in a similar manner.

   Lo-Ruhamah: meaning "not pitied" or "not loved" (1:6), indicating that God will no longer forgive or have pity on Israel. Judah, by contrast, he will save. (This comes to pass in 722 BC, when Israel is defeated and exiled by Assyria; Judah is delivered from Assyria in 701 BC.)

   Lo-Ammi: meaning "not my people"—"for you are not my people and I am not your God" (1:9). That is the reverse of the covenant formula, in which God says, "I will be your God, and you shall be my people" (Jeremiah 7:23); it indicates that the covenant has been broken.

---

1 The Hebrew word for "harlotry," in both its verb and noun forms *(zanah, zanun)* can also mean adultery or idolatry.

2 Note: *Jezreel,* which means "scattered by God," is the name of the valley where Jehu slaughtered the royal family and usurped the throne of Israel prior to the time of Hosea. The king at the time of Hosea, Jeroboam II, is fourth of that line of kings.

c. *Is there any hope that the judgments contained in these names might be reversed? (See* ***1:10–2:1*** *and* ***CCC 211.****)*

Although the meaning of the third child's name sounds devastatingly final, there is hope. Verses 10-11 recall an earlier covenant than Sinai, one in which God promised Abraham to make his descendants as numerous as the sands on the seashore (see Genesis 22:17). Hosea goes on to say that all the names ultimately will be reversed. Jezreel will figure in a new and great day; instead of "God scatters," God will, in a sense, "sow" them in the land, and in that very place, they will be made again "my people," and "she has obtained pity." How can God do this for a nation that has forsaken him? The *Catechism* states: "The divine name, 'I AM' or 'He Is,' expresses God's faithfulness: despite the faithlessness of men's sin and the punishment it deserves, he keeps 'steadfast love for thousands'" (CCC 211; Exodus 34:7).

2. *Re-read* ***2:1-13,*** *where Hosea first states his case against Gomer (verses 1-7) and then unites it to God's charge against Israel in verses 8-13. What are some of Israel's chief sins? What does God say he will do about them?*

   As Gomer goes after other men, Israel has gone after the gods of other nations, believing them to be the source of their goods and prosperity (see verses 5, 8-9, and 13). They have even turned to worshiping Baal. Therefore, God will take away those things they seek to gain, which are really provided by him—the God who sends the rain and brings life—and will put an end to their idolatrous feasting.

3. *Now read* ***2:14-23.***

   a. *What is the ultimate motivation behind God's decision to withdraw his support from Israel?*

   God's discipline always has the purpose of purifying and drawing his people back to himself. This is "tough love," allowing Israel to face the consequences of putting its trust in idols so that it will remember him and turn back to him. God's ultimate goal is to return to the intimacy of the early days of their love, to restore Israel to a relationship with him alone.

   b. *Describe the New Covenant God will make for them if they return.*

   The New Covenant will be everlasting (verse 19). Its hallmarks will be righteousness, justice, steadfast love, and mercy. There will be no more infidelity. They will be betrothed "in faithfulness" and will "know the LORD" (verse 20). The renewed covenant will overflow in blessings on all of creation (verse 18), on the land and nations. The wars that have been troubling them will be gone, and they will be safe. Thus, a complete reversal is possible if Israel "answers" God (verse 15). This is summarized in the reversal of names in verse 23. God says, "I will have pity on Not pitied, and I will say to Not my people, 'You are my people'; and he shall say, 'Thou art my God.'" Israel will then be back in a covenant relationship with the LORD.

Infidelity and Consequences (Hosea 4:1–14:1)

4. *Starting in Chapter 4, Hosea addresses the people of Israel directly. "The LORD has a controversy with the inhabitants of the land," he says in the first verse. This is legal terminology that implies a lawsuit over the broken Sinai covenant, in which Israel swore to follow only God and to keep his commands, which was a "marriage moment" between the LORD and his people.*

   In 4:1, we read, "There is no faithfulness or kindness, and no knowledge of God in the land." According to verses 2-3, what are the consequences of the lack of these things in the lives of the people?

As a result of there being no faithfulness, kindness, or knowledge of God, the "land mourns" (verse 3). The litany of sins in 4:2 reads like the reverse of the Ten Commandments received on Mount Sinai. There is "swearing, lying, killing, stealing, and committing adultery; they break all bounds and murder follows murder." Their sin even affects the land and animals, as creation is characterized as languishing and the land as mourning.

5. *Hosea 4:6 says that Israel is "destroyed for lack of knowledge." The words "to know" and "knowledge of God" appear frequently in Hosea.*[3]

   a. *Consider the following verses, and record what you discover about the importance of "knowing" and "knowledge of God."*

   Hosea 2:20: *What is the basis of knowing God?*

   Hosea describes knowing God as an outcome of a committed relationship ("betrothal") with God that is rooted in God's righteousness, justice, steadfast love, mercy, and faithfulness.

   Hosea 4:6: *What is the result of "lack of knowledge" of God?*

   The lack of knowledge of God has taken a tremendous toll on the people, who God says are "destroyed" as a consequence. Note that in the rest of the sixth verse, "lack of knowledge" is described in another way as having "forgotten the law of your God." We can see, then, that "knowing God" is much more than being acquainted with him. It has to do with knowing and following his Law.

   b. ***Think About It:*** *It is sobering to learn that roughly one-third of Catholics in the United States believe that God is merely an "impersonal force" rather than a personal Being with whom we can have a relationship.*[4] *What might that lack of the "knowledge of God" mean for attitudes and actions in our society? Do you see anything from Hosea's day reflected in our day?*

   Answers will vary; encourage discussion.

6. *In Hosea 2:19, God says he will betroth Israel to him "in steadfast love." The Hebrew word he uses,* hesed, *appears six times in Hosea, always in reference to the covenant faithfulness of the* Lord. *When Israel breaks that covenant, ending God's "legal" obligation to honor it, God's* hesed *reveals "its deeper aspect: It showed itself as what it was at the beginning, that is, as love that gives, love more powerful than betrayal, grace stronger than sin."*[5]

   a. *Read* **Hosea 6:6.** *What does God require of his people in return for his* hesed?

   God requires that the people return his love. True worship is found in steadfast love and the "knowledge of God," not in the externals of sacrificial offerings. This is not to say that offerings are bad. After all, God commanded them. But to be acceptable, they must be made from the heart.

   b. ***New Testament Connection:*** *Jesus quotes Hosea 6:6 twice in the Gospel of Matthew. Read* **Matthew 9:10-13.**[6] *How does Jesus apply Hosea's words to his day?*

[3] In Hebrew, the word *yadah*, "to know," means more than simply realizing or understanding something. It is based on experience or relationship and includes acting on knowledge. It can even refer to intimate sexual knowledge, as in Genesis 4:1, when Adam "knew" his wife. Similarly, "knowledge of God" *(da'at elohim)* means not just knowing about God but having a close and committed relationship with him, like a husband and wife.

[4] Pew Religious Forum on Religion & Public Life, "U.S. Religious Landscape Survey" (2008), as quoted in Sherry Weddell, *Forming Intentional Disciples: The Path to Knowing and Following Jesus* (Huntington, IN: Our Sunday Visitor, 2012), 43-44.

[5] St. John Paul II, *Dives in Misericordia* 4, note 52.

[6] Hosea 6:6 is also quoted in Matthew 12:7.

Hosea 6:6 strikes at the heart of what is most important in following God, which is to be like him and show mercy. Where the Pharisees condemned tax collectors and sinners, Jesus judges them to be in need of healing. Only by learning the meaning of Hosea's words would the Pharisees understand why Jesus ate with people with whom it was unlawful for him to share a meal.

The Father's Love (Hosea 11)

7. *Read **Hosea 11,** in which another metaphor is used to describe God's love for Israel. What is that metaphor? What does it teach us about God's heart and the motivation behind his actions?*

   God is pictured as a loving Father, calling his son out of Egypt and raising him as his own. Israel is that firstborn son, who fails to return the Father's love and turns to other gods instead. God, with his father's heart, is in anguish (verses 8-9). Yet he cannot give his child over to be destroyed. His motive for letting Israel go back into slavery and for holding back his anger and restoring them when they return to him is love and compassion.

   Note: Many years later, Jesus does what Israel has failed to do. As the true firstborn Son, he is called out of Egypt to lead the people on a new Exodus into the true Promised Land of the kingdom of God.

8. **Catechism *Connection:*** *We are not that different today than Israel was. Read **CCC 2787,** and comment on what the Church has to say about our relationship with God.*

   We call God "Father" because the promises he has made to his people Israel—including the promise that he will be our God and we will be his people—are fulfilled in the New Covenant in his Son, Jesus Christ. He reaches out to us in love, and we respond with love and faithfulness. Hosea describes God's love for Israel as being like that a father; in the Son, we *are* God's children.

A Plea to Return (Hosea 14)

9. *Hosea 12–13 details the many sins of Ephraim (Israel). The chapters end in loss and in the terrible judgment that will result from the people turning from God to foreign nations; but immediately after them comes a call to conversion. Read **Hosea 14:1-8,** and answer the following questions.*

   a. *In verses 1-3, what does Hosea call on Israel to do?*

      Hosea calls on the people of Israel to return to the Lord and repent, asking him to take away their sin. He also asks them to "render the fruit of [their] lips"—in other words, to stop saying "our God" to idols and to praise the true God instead.

   b. *What does God promise to do and be for the people in verses 4, 5, and 8?*

      God will turn his anger away from them, heal their faithlessness, and love them freely. He will be like dew to them, providing refreshment, fruit, and nourishment.

   c. *What advantages will these things have for Israel (verses 5-7)?*

      Having returned to God and received healing, Israel will blossom, take root, grow, and become beautiful, fragrant, and fruitful. God's people will return to his care, dwell beneath his shadow, and flourish and blossom.

10. *Imagine—God has plentiful grounds for "divorce," yet he asks to be reconciled. After all the people of Israel have done to him, how can he take them back? Read **CCC 218,** and comment on what you learn.*

God's love is not dependent on the worthiness of the people of Israel. He continues to reach out to them, call them back, and pardon them because of "his sheer gratuitous love" (CCC 218).[7] That should give us hope. Pope Francis says, "The Lord never tires of forgiving: never! It is we who tire of asking his forgiveness. Let us ask for the grace not to tire of asking for forgiveness, because he never tires of forgiving."[8]

D. Application

Facilitators: If time allows, have group members share their responses to the following application question.

Think back over what you have learned. In what sense are you his *child and is God* your *Father? In what sense do you "know" God? In other words, what kind of relationship do you have with him? What part of Hosea's message speaks to you most—for yourself, for your family, or for those around you?*

After the small-group discussion, watch Thomas Smith's video presentation on *Session 2* – Hosea: Living God's Love Story.

7 See Deuteronomy 4:37, 7:8, 10:15.

8 Pope Francis, March 17, 2013, homily in Vatican City.

Facilitators: Read these recommended responses to the questions ahead of time to help you prepare to lead the small-group discussion.

Participants: Reinforce what you have learned by reviewing these recommended responses after the small-group discussion and before you continue to the next session.

A. Establish the Context

Facilitators: Take a moment to establish the context and what was learned in the previous session.

B. Read the Story

Facilitators: If there is time, have someone read each passage aloud before it is discussed.

C. Take a Deeper Look

The Reluctant Prophet (Jonah 1)

1. *When the word of the Lord comes to the prophet Jonah, telling him to cry out against the "great city" of Nineveh because of its wickedness, Jonah's response is to flee on a ship to Tarshish.*

   a. *Find Joppa, Jonah's starting point, on the map on page 26. Locate Nineveh, where he is asked to go, and Tarshish, where he decides to go instead. What do you notice?*

   Tarshish is in the opposite direction from where God asks Jonah to go. To the people in Canaan of Jonah's day, Tarshish was the farthest trading port and represented the very "ends of the earth."

   b. *Jonah's reluctance to go to Nineveh is understandable in light of Assyria's fearsome, tyrannical rule. Yet, it is not Nineveh he seems to be afraid of. From what does Jonah flee, according to verses 2, 3, and 10?*

   As the author takes pains to tell us three times, Jonah flees from the "presence [literally, "face"] of the Lord." He does not want to carry God's message.

   c. *Read* ***Genesis 3:8 and 4:16.*** *Who else have we seen flee in this way? How were their circumstances similar to or different from Jonah's?*

   Adam and Eve hid from God's presence after eating from the Tree of Knowledge. Cain left God's presence after being dismayed at his punishment for Abel's murder. While these people fled God's presence because they sinned, Jonah flees to avoid obeying God's command.

2. *Compare and contrast Jonah's response to God's Word to the response of the captain, the mariners, the fish, the wind, and the sea. Note the verses where you find your answers.*

   Everyone and everything obeys the Lord—except Jonah. In contrast to Jonah's frightened flight, the wind and the sea obey the Lord, breaking into "a mighty tempest" (verses 4, 13) on his command and ceasing when the sailors do what they believe the Lord to be asking (verse 15). The captain and the mariners seek the Lord's will when their cries to their gods fail, and they throw Jonah overboard only as a last resort (verse 14); even in their fear, they believe Jonah's word is of God (verses 12, 14). They also offer sacrifices and make vows to God when the storm ends. Finally, the fish "appointed" by the LORD swallows the hapless prophet on command and then vomits him out again (see 2:10).

3. *Describe the progressive downward spiral that parallels Jonah's trip "away from the presence of the LORD" in **1:3, 1:5, 1:15, 1:17, 2:5, and 2:6a** (NAB: 1:3, 1:5, 1:15, 2:1, 2:6, and 2:7a).*

   Every step Jonah takes away from God is described as heading "down" toward death. Jonah goes "down" to Joppa (1:3), then "down into the inner part of the ship," where he lies down to sleep (1:5). The men throw him into the sea (1:15), and he goes down into the belly of a great fish (1:17), which takes him into the deep (2:5), to "the roots of the mountains" (i.e., the bottom of the sea, 2:6), and finally the bars of "the Pit" close upon him, seemingly forever (2:6).

4. *Read **Psalm 139:1-12.***

   a. *How is the truth of this psalm reflected in Jonah 1?*

   Psalm 139 is a beautiful hymn to the all-seeing, all-knowing love of God for each one of us. However far one goes, whatever one does, one can never flee from his presence. His Spirit is in heaven, in Sheol, at the ends of the sea, in the morning, and in the darkest dark—nothing is dark enough or far enough to hide us from him. Jonah discovers this as he attempts to flee God's presence to the ends of the earth (Tarshish).

   b. *How have you experienced the far-reaching persistence of God's love?*

   Encourage one or more participants to share their experience.

God Gets Jonah's Attention (Jonah 2)

5. *Read **Jonah 2.** In verse 1 (NAB: verse 2), we read that Jonah prays from the belly of the fish. How does Jonah describe the place from which he cries to God in verses 1-6 (NAB: verses 2-7)?*

   Jonah says he called to the LORD "out of my distress" and "out of the belly of Sheol" (literally, "out of the grave"). He has sought to flee the presence of the LORD, and he finds himself in grave distress, feeling as though waters are closing in over his head. He is drowning and feels the end of his life coming on him.

6. *Describe Jonah's prayer in 2:1-9 (NAB: 2:2-10) as it reflects his change of heart.*

   Jonah begins in distress but remembers the LORD and is moved to pray, which changes his lament to confidence and praise. Contrasting himself with those who "forsake their true loyalty" (verse 8), Jonah vows to make a sacrifice of thanksgiving to the LORD. His prayer is cast in the past tense; in his bold affirmation that, "Deliverance belongs to the LORD!" (verse 9), Jonah declares what he knows to be true regardless of his current situation.

7. *Recall the many times Jonah has "gone down" lower and lower, away from the LORD (see your response to question 3). What is God's response to Jonah's distress? See **verse 6** (NAB: verse 7).*

   Even in the depths of the sea, Jonah cannot escape the LORD's presence. In fact, it is here in the belly of the fish, in extreme isolation and separation, that God gets Jonah's attention. God allows Jonah's fall to draw him back to himself. Jonah goes down, and God lifts him up from the pit.

God Calls Jonah Again (Jonah 3)

8. *Read **Jonah 3.** Given the reputation of the people of Nineveh, one might expect their reaction to Jonah's message to be similar to the reaction Lot's sons-in-law had to God's message that the city of Sodom would be destroyed (see **Genesis 19**): Lot's family thought he was joking and had to be forcibly removed to be saved.*

   a. *Describe the response of the people of Nineveh to Jonah.*

   The people of Nineveh believe God. Without protest, objection, or reluctance, they don sackcloth (typically a sign of mourning, an act of penance, or a means of pleading for God's deliverance) and proclaim a fast.

   b. *Describe the response of the king and his motivation in verses 6-10. How would you compare him with the captain in 1:6? What does each know about God?*

   The king of Nineveh responds immediately by donning the public signs of mourning (sackcloth and ashes) and declaring a fast for all people and their flocks. It is a wholehearted fast by all with the expressed intent of turning away from violence, throwing themselves on God's mercy, and asking him to save them. In a similar way, the captain in 1:6 asks Jonah to call on his God in hopes he will save them. The captain and the king both act without knowing whether God will respond. But they seem to know instinctively what Jonah learned in the belly of the fish: "Deliverance belongs to the LORD!" (2:9).

9. *How is the prophecy from **Jeremiah 18:7-8** borne out in God's response to Nineveh's repentance?*

   Jeremiah's prophecy to the people of Israel that if a nation on which God has declared destruction for its wickedness turns from evil, he also will turn from the evil he intended for that nation. This promise includes the pagan nations. The story of Nineveh bears this out: When the people of Nineveh turn from their evil, God turns away from his plans to destroy them.

10. ***New Testament Connection:** Read **Matthew 12:38-42.** What meaning does Jesus give Jonah's story in applying it to his generation?*

    Jesus, who is faced with "an evil and adulterous generation" that seeks a sign in order to believe, gives only the "sign of Jonah" (Matthew 12:39, NAB) who was three days and nights in the belly of the whale. Similarly, Jesus will be buried three days and nights before rising again. Whereas the wicked men of Nineveh repent at Jonah's preaching, Jesus' generation is condemned for not listening to him—even though he is far greater than Jonah.

God Gets Jonah's Attention Again (Jonah 4)

11. ***Think About It:** When Jonah says, "I knew that thou art a gracious God and merciful, slow to anger, and abounding in steadfast love" (4:2), he is quoting God's own words in Exodus 34:6-7. In that passage, God declared his mercy in the context of Israel turning from him to the Golden Calf even as he was establishing his covenant with them. In spite of their wickedness, God forgave them and took them as his own. Knowing this about God, why is Jonah angry? How can he use these words to justify his flight to Tarshish?*

    Those words were for Israel. It is a great leap for Jonah to believe they apply also to the pagan nations, especially to an enemy as feared and wicked as Assyria. He can hardly believe God would forgive Nineveh, and now he has been made a fool—his words of doom have not come to pass. (According to Deuteronomy 18:22, a prophet can be judged to be true only when his words come to pass.) He sulks off and watches to see whether God means what he has said.

It is tragically ironic that Israel, throughout the Old Testament, does not repent, yet pagan Nineveh does. This is a staggering contrast. After hearing Jonah's brief message, everyone from the king down immediately turns from their sins and lies in sackcloth and ashes.

12. a. Jonah would rather die than carry God's message of mercy to Nineveh. Now, in Chapter 4, he asks to die rather than witness this mercy. Explain how God gets Jonah's attention in verses 6-9.

Just as God sends a "great fish" to swallow Jonah, capturing his attention mid-flight and effectively saving him from himself, he now appoints a plant, a worm, and a sultry east wind to draw Jonah's attention in the midst of his anger. The plant—which God causes to rise up and shade Jonah, then wither, exposing him to the heat—is contrasted to Nineveh: If a plant is so worthy of concern, how much more worthy the people of Nineveh!

b. What message does God intend Jonah to learn from this? (See ***verses 10-11.****)*

God uses the plant to grab Jonah's attention and drive home a message. Jonah is "angry enough to die" over the death of the plant. Can he not therefore understand God's pity for a city of 120,000, whose inhabitants "do not know their right hand from their left"? This phrase recalls Jesus' words from the Cross: "Father, forgive them; for they know not what they do" (Luke 23:34). God has pity on those who do not know him.

The humorous conclusion of the book bears an additional message for Jonah. He may not think much of the people of Nineveh or their livestock, but God is compassionate toward them. Their repentance contrasts greatly with the obstinate disobedience of Judah and Israel.

Notice that in his unwillingness to extend mercy to pagans, Jonah is a microcosm of Israel. Chosen to carry God's light to the nations, Israel is intended to be a messenger of reconciliation to them. Not only does it fail in that vocation, Israel rejects it altogether. Israel throws herself to the nations like Jonah has himself thrown into the sea. But God is not limited by Jonah's unwillingness to speak, and he will not be limited by the shortcomings of his people. God's message of mercy begins with Jonah himself. It is Jonah's life and story more than his words that proclaims the message God has for his people.

D. Application

Facilitators: If time allows, have group members share their responses to the following application question.

Have you ever run (or are you running now) from God? Or is there someone you think does not deserve mercy? Who is it? What prevents you from bearing God's message to them or showing them mercy? With this in mind, what lesson or lessons can you take from Jonah and apply in that situation?

After the small-group discussion, watch Thomas Smith's video presentation on *Session 3* – Jonah: God's Reluctant Messenger.

Session 4 – Responses

Isaiah Part 1 – Prophet of Woe

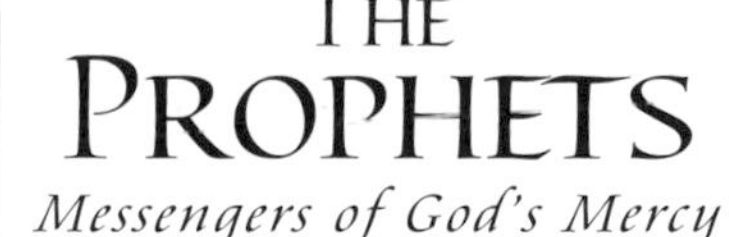

Facilitators: *Read these recommended responses to the questions ahead of time to help you prepare to lead the small-group discussion.*

Participants: *Reinforce what you have learned by reviewing these recommended responses after the small-group discussion and before you continue to the next session.*

A. Establish the Context

Facilitators: Take a moment to establish the context and what was learned in the previous session.

B. Read the Story

Facilitators: If there is time, have someone read each passage aloud before it is discussed.

C. Take a Deeper Look

God Reasons with Israel and Calls for Repentance (Isaiah 1)

1. *In 1:2-4, "The LORD" (literally, "YHWH," the God who established a covenant with his people) lays out his case against Judah.*

   a. *What are the charges?*

   The "sons" God has raised (in 1:3, he calls them "my people") have rebelled against him. Despite their covenant relationship with God, they neither know him nor understand him. Not only are they sinful and corrupt, they have turned from God to the point of utter estrangement.

   b. *Compare these charges to the charges God levels against Israel in* ***Hosea 4:1-6.*** *How are they similar? Why is this significant? (See questions 4-6 in Session 2.)*

   Hosea chastises the people of Israel because there is "no faithfulness or kindness, and no knowledge of God in the land" (4:1). The land and its inhabitants, even the animals, languish under the weight of the sin (4:2-3). "My people are destroyed for lack of knowledge; because [they] have rejected knowledge" and have forgotten God's Law (4:6). Now Isaiah says that the people of Judah do not know or understand God. In the previous session, we saw that "knowledge" means more than simply knowing *about* God; it describes a faithful relationship with him. Like Israel before, Judah has broken its covenant relationship with God.

2. *The sacrifices Hosea condemns in Israel are made at false altars to false gods (see* ***Hosea 2:13 and 8:13****). In Isaiah 1, God rejects Judah's sacrifices made to him in the Temple in Jerusalem. Why? (See* ***Isaiah 1:12-15,*** *and read* ***CCC 2100*** *for insight into this question.)*

   Judah's sacrifices in Isaiah 1:13 are not wrong but are "vain" (i.e., ineffective). Why? Because the people's "hands are full of blood" (verse 15). They persist in doing evil and opposing God's laws. No number of sacrifices can make up for the fact that they do not reflect an internal offering. The *Catechism* draws attention to this key message of the Old Testament prophets—exemplified here in Isaiah—that ritual observance means nothing if it does not reflect true "knowledge of God" manifested in a living relationship (see CCC 2100).

3. *God lays two paths before his people in Isaiah 1:18-20. What are the two paths, and where do they lead? (See also **verse 27.**)*

   While Judah's behavior has set it on the road to destruction, God graciously offers an alternate way. The LORD says, "Come now, let us reason together … though your sins are like scarlet, they shall be as white as snow" (1:18). Red dyes are notoriously difficult to remove. Here we see that even the deepest stains of sin can be removed if the people are willing and obedient—that is, if they will repent and turn from evil to do good. This path will bring them goodness and prosperity; but if they continue as they are, like traitorous "harlots" (verse 21), they will be destroyed.

4. ***Think About It:*** *What does the first chapter of Isaiah reveal about God's heart and desire?*

   God is "the LORD" (i.e., "YHWH," the great "I AM"), who has made a covenant with his people to be their God and make them his treasured possession if they will but follow him (see Deuteronomy 7:6). Not surprisingly, the LORD takes the sinful actions of the people personally (i.e., as a rebellion against the established relationship they have with him). He speaks as a father to a rebellious but still-loved child with what today we might call "tough love." It is a love that burns hotly against their destructive behavior and declares without apology the logical end of such behavior: violence and destruction. It is a love that pleads for the loved ones to wake up to those consequences and turn back, repent, and change—and receive the life he promises them.

The Call of Isaiah (Isaiah 6)

5. *Read **Isaiah 6:1-8.***

   a. *Consider the details of Isaiah's vision. What do they tell you about God?*

   The LORD sits like a priest and king upon a heavenly throne, "high and lifted up; and his train filled the Temple" (verse 1). He is surrounded with angels and echoes of praise: He is thrice holy and his glory cannot be contained but fills the earth. This is a glorious picture, far beyond that of any earthly ruler. His voice sounds like thunder, shaking the foundations of the Temple and filling it with smoke and the overwhelming presence of the holy. His glory easily eclipses all earthly powers.

   b. ***New Testament Connection:*** *Centuries later, the apostle John is given a similar vision in Revelation 4:1-8. What similarities do you see between the two descriptions?*

   John provides more details, but the essential elements are the same. The vision is of heaven. God is seated on his throne, and he is such a glorious sight that he cannot be described directly. His glory must be inferred from his surroundings. Thunder, fire, and smoke are present, and heavenly creatures and angels ceaselessly sing, "Holy, Holy, Holy," as they praise the Lord.

   c. *Think about what the angels say in this passage. Does it sound familiar? At what part of the Mass do we enter into this angelic praise of God's holiness? What do we say?*

   In the preface acclamation (traditionally known as the *Sanctus*) of the Eucharistic Prayer, we ask that our voices be joined with those of angels in their heavenly worship as together we proclaim:

Holy, Holy, Holy Lord, God of hosts.
Heaven and earth are full of your glory.
Hosanna in the highest.
Blessed is he who comes in the name of the Lord.
Hosanna in the highest.

6. *Read all of* ***Isaiah 6.***

   a. *Based on this chapter, what kind of a man is Isaiah?*

   Isaiah is a man who has visions from the LORD. When he experiences these visions, he is consumed with an awareness of his own sin and of the uncleanness and unworthiness of himself and his people before all-holy God. He is humble, willing, and obedient: He hears the voice of the LORD and listens. He replies, "Here am I! Send me" (verse 8). He has a heart for the people, evident in his cry of, "How long, O LORD?" (verse 11).

   b. ***Think About It:*** *What might be discouraging or encouraging about the details of Isaiah's calling? Is there encouragement in the fact that he himself is cleansed?*

   Isaiah is charged with carrying God's message to a people who are hard of heart (who will neither listen nor understand) and to continue proclaiming this message even to what seems like the end, when the people are carried off into exile. How discouraging that must be for Isaiah—to know that they will not repent but to persist in giving them the chance. There is a glimmer of hope in the mention of the stump that will remain—"the holy seed" (verse 13). All is not lost while seeds remain to be replanted.

   Another ray of hope and encouragement can be seen in Isaiah's call itself, which is part of his written message. Isaiah himself is "lost" and "unclean" (verse 5), part and parcel with the nation. Yet God takes away his guilt and forgives his sin and sends him, clean, to bear his love song to the people. In this, Isaiah is a microcosm of the nation that God also desires to forgive, clean, and send.

7. **Catechism *Connection:*** *Read* ***CCC 208,*** *and consider what you have read in Isaiah 6. What ramification does the holiness of God have for people who are separated from him by sin?*

   While God's absolute holiness makes people keenly aware of how very *unholy* they are, and while the first reaction of the human mind is to hide from his presence and expect judgment (examples include not just Isaiah, but Moses and Peter), it is a blessed paradox that the very holiness of God means he can forgive. In his holiness, "God is greater than our hearts" (1 John 3:19-20).

"The LORD Himself Will Give You a Sign" (Isaiah 7:14)

8. *By the days of King Ahaz, Judah is in crisis. Israel (Ephraim)*[1] *and Syria have joined against Assyria, and they are attempting to force Judah to join their revolt. As an alternative, Ahaz enters into a protection treaty with Assyria, requiring Judah vassals to pay tribute to and worship Assyrian gods.*[2] *Isaiah is a court prophet with Ahaz's ear, and he speaks to him for the LORD. Read* ***Isaiah 7:1-9.*** *What message does he bring?*

---

1 "Ephraim," the name of the largest tribe in the north, was sometimes used to refer to the entire Northern Kingdom, Israel. "The house of David" in verse 2, refers to the kingdom of Judah.

2 See 2 Kings 16:7, 10-18.

Through Isaiah, God tells Ahaz not to fear Syria and Ephraim (Israel), whose plot to depose him will not come to pass. He says that within sixty-five years, Ephraim will be shattered and no longer a people.

9. *This message bears with it the hope that Ahaz will put his trust in God and not in political alliances. Isaiah asks Ahaz to request a sign—which he refuses to do. But God himself gives Ahaz a sign for the house of David. Read* ***Isaiah 7:10-17.***

   a. *The sign is a familiar one. Describe it and the One who is promised.*

   The sign that comes from the Lord is the birth to a young virgin of a son called "Emmanuel," which means "God with us." Before the child is very old, the two kings feared by Ahaz will be conquered and their lands deserted. As an image of God in their midst, the child is a sign that points to future judgment on a non-repentant Judah. For this reason, he will become a sanctuary to those who turn to him and "a stone of offense," or "snare," to those who rebel (see 8:14).

   b. *The sign of a coming child echoes through the next few chapters. Read* ***Isaiah 9:6-7*** *(NAB: 9:5-6). What role and characteristics will this child have?*

   The child will be "given" to them by God, and he will restore and establish God's kingdom. He will govern it and the world in everlasting peace, justice, and righteousness from a seat on the eternal throne of David. (This describes one who will fulfill God's covenant promise to David in 2 Samuel 7.) He will have great titles befitting a King sent from God who is literally "God with us": "Wonderful Counselor, Mighty God, Everlasting Father, Prince of Peace."

10. *In Isaiah 11:1, the expected Savior-child is described as "a shoot from the stump of Jesse" (i.e., a King from the royal line of Jesse's son David, which will have been cut off by that time).*

   a. *Read* ***11:2-5,*** *and list the characteristics of this future anointed King.*

   The spirit of the Lord will rest upon God's King with wisdom and understanding, counsel and might, and knowledge and the fear of the Lord. He will delight in the fear of the Lord and will judge with righteousness and faithfulness.

   b. *Read* ***11:10-12, 16.***[3] *What will this "root of Jesse" accomplish?*

   The "root of Jesse" will restore the people of God, gathering them from the four corners of the earth. Their restoration will be similar to their exodus from Egypt. The remnant will return to the Promised Land from captivity. This prophecy has multiple layers of fulfillment. First, Judah will return home from Babylonian captivity. But the ultimate fulfillment will come many years later when Jesus Christ, the "root of Jesse," will free all people from their bondage to sin and restore them to the true "promised land" of his heavenly kingdom.

Hezekiah's Victory (Isaiah 36–39)

11. *In 701 BC, Sennacherib brings his huge Assyrian army to the gates of Jerusalem and the "Rabshakeh" (called the "the commander" in the NAB) delivers a message.*

   a. *Read* ***Isaiah 36:13-20.*** *What challenge does Isaiah bring to the people?*

[3] Note: In Isaiah 11:10, "stand as an ensign" ("set up as a signal" in the NAB) means to put up a banner or raise a flag for the nations to gather around.

Sennacherib's spokesman delivers a direct challenge to the LORD and Hezekiah from "the great king" (36:13) of Assyria, saying that Hezekiah is not to be trusted. "Do not let Hezekiah make you rely on the LORD" (36:15), he challenges, because no other king or god has been able to deliver its people yet from Assyria. Instead, Sennacherib offers peace and security under his rule.

b. *Now read Hezekiah's response to this challenge in* ***37:1-4 and 37:14-20*** *(where he responds when it comes a second time). Explain how Hezekiah lives up to his name, which means, "God is my strength."*

Hezekiah does what previous kings have failed to do. Rather than capitulating to Assyria or seeking foreign aid, he goes into mourning and turns directly to God in prayer. It is significant that he sees very clearly that God has ultimate sovereignty (37:16) and that Assyria's threats are not so much against Jerusalem as they are against God himself (37:4, 17). He sees that the reason Assyria has triumphed over other nations is that their gods were not gods but idols. Now Assyria threatens the living God, and Hezekiah prays to the LORD, the one true God, for deliverance.

c. *Read* ***37:33-38.*** *What is the result? What does this say about God?*

For his own sake and for that of his promise to David, the LORD determines not only to defend Jerusalem, but to keep Assyria from even coming near it. The result is an astonishing, incontrovertible demonstration of God's power. During the night, with no human intervention, the giant Assyrian army is destroyed by an angel of the LORD. Sennacherib escapes only to be killed later by his own sons as Isaiah prophesied in 37:7. The Assyrian threat is over.

D. Application

Facilitators: If time allows, have group members share their responses to the following application question.

Do you wonder where Hezekiah finds the strength of faith he needs to face Sennacherib? Isaiah 38 gives us a clue. A year prior to the Assyrian invasion, Hezekiah's fervent prayers on his deathbed had brought him personal healing and a reprieve for the nation: fifteen additional years of life and a promise that God would deliver him and Jerusalem from Assyria. His beautiful prayer of thanksgiving and devotion to the LORD is recorded there as well. Spend some time reading this chapter and meditating on it. Has there been a time in your life when God has intervened on your behalf? Can this strengthen you for future battles?

After the small-group discussion, watch Thomas Smith's video presentation on *Session 4* – Isaiah Part 1: Prophet of Woe.

Session 5 – Responses

Isaiah Part 2 – Prophet of Consolation

Facilitators: *Read these recommended responses to the questions ahead of time to help you prepare to lead the small-group discussion.*

Participants: *Reinforce what you have learned by reviewing these recommended responses after the small-group discussion and before you continue to the next session.*

A. Establish the Context

Facilitators: Take a moment to establish the context and what was learned in the previous session.

B. Read the Story

Facilitators: If there is time, have someone read each passage aloud before it is discussed.

C. Take a Deeper Look

"Comfort My People": Restoration Promised (Isaiah 40–41)

1. *Recall that Isaiah begins in 1:2 with God's complaint against his rebellious sons. All through the years of Judah's rebellion and lack of repentance, God's message is "woe." Read* ***Isaiah 40:1-2.*** *Now that they are years into captivity, what is God's message to them?*

   God's message to his people in their captivity is one of consolation. He asks his prophet to speak tender words of comfort to his people to let them know they have been fully punished for their sins. Their warfare is over, and their sins are pardoned.

2. *From the time of the Exodus, God has promised to be with his people and to dwell among them. This is signified by his presence in the Holy of Holies in the Temple. In 587 BC, though, the Temple is destroyed. Now God's people are in exile, and they may wonder where he is. Read* ***Isaiah 40:3-11.*** *What good news is Isaiah asked to cry out to the people of Judah to bring them comfort?*

   The good news is nothing less than the end of their exile. God is coming in glory to be with them. The preparations called for in verses 3-5 are like the preparations made to clear the way for a king's triumphant entry into a city. "Behold your God!" is to be shouted from the heights (verse 9). Their God, whom they abandoned in Judah and who thus abandoned them to Babylon, is returning in power to rule and reward them (verse 10), feed and gather them, and lead them home (verse 11).

3. a. *For many generations, the people of Judah have witnessed firsthand the terrible power of nations that stand in defiance to God and against them. Read* ***Isaiah 40:12-31.*** *Who is the LORD, that they should listen to his call, let alone trust him and obey?*

   God created everything (verse 12). He is the source of wisdom and understanding (verses 13-14). The nations "are as nothing" before his power (verses 15-17); other gods (idols) are merely the creations of men, capable of nothing. No other power can compare with that of the LORD (verses

18-27). With unwavering strength, God will give power and might to those who have none and strength, support, and refreshment to those who wait upon him (verses 28-31).

b. *In what ways have you experienced God's strength and support in your life? How do these verses speak to you?*

Encourage discussion as time allows.

4. ***New Testament Connection:*** *There are sometimes "layers" of fulfillment to prophecies, each pointing to something beyond the last. The immediate fulfillment of Isaiah's prophecy will be when Judah is rescued from Babylon and allowed to return to the Promised Land of Israel. According to* **Matthew 3:1-3,** *to what future "rescue" and "return" do Isaiah's words point? Who will pick up the cry of the voice heard in Isaiah 40:3?*

In the ultimate fulfillment, all humanity will be rescued from sin and brought to the "promised land" of heaven. St. John the Baptist later takes up the cry of the voice heard in Isaiah 41:3, proclaiming the coming of Jesus who will lead his people into the kingdom of heaven.

"Behold My Servant": Agents of Restoration (Isaiah 42–55)

5. *In the following chart, read each of the four Servant Songs, and record what you learn about the Servant's identity, character, and mission.*

Facilitators: Jesus fulfilled the messianic hope of Israel in his threefold office of Priest, Prophet, and King (see CCC 436). It is interesting to see those roles reflected in the Servant Songs, as noted under "The Servant's Mission" in the chart below.

Servant Song in Isaiah	The Servant's Identity and Character	The Servant's Mission
42:1-4	One whom God chooses, upholds, delights in, and upon whom he puts his Spirit. He is humble, gentle, faithful, and persistent.	To bring forth justice and establish justice on earth. – This is the role of a **king.**
49:1-6	Created, called, and named for this purpose by God; speaks with God's authority: "Listen to me" (verse 1); "sharp" and "polished" like a weapon, ready and effective; hidden away until now.	To speak the Word of God; to glorify God in himself; to restore Israel to himself; and to be a light to the nations so God's salvation will extend to the whole world. – To speak God's Word to the people and nations is the role of a **prophet.**
50:4-9	Spokesman who speaks God's Word; listens to God and obeys, and trusts him to the victorious end, even through suffering; bold in God's power; does not shrink back when persecuted but perseveres; knows God will come to his aid.	Speaks words to sustain the weary; does what God asks of him. – Here, the Servant fills the role of a **teacher** by word and example.

Continued on next page

Continued from previous page

Servant Song in Isaiah	The Servant's Identity and Character	The Servant's Mission
52:13–53:12	Prosperous, exalted, lifted up, and yet disfigured, despised, full of sorrow, rejected; meek in affliction, obedient to the Father's will even to death; sinless himself but an offering for sin for others.	To bear the grief and sorrows of his people; to intercede for and bear the punishment for their sin so that they might be healed. As a consequence of his death, many will be accounted righteous, and he shall be victorious. – By interceding, he fills the role of a **priest.**

6. *Each of the Servant Songs is followed by a kind of unfolding or expansion of the song, like a commentary. These verses speak of the effects or significance of the Servant's work. Read the following passages along with the comments you made above and write what you learn from the commentary verses.*

Servant Song "Commentary" in Isaiah	The Significance or Results of the Servant's Work
42:5-20	God calls the Servant to be "a covenant to the people, a light to the nations" (verse 6), to open blind eyes and free prisoners. Through him, God declares "new things" (verse 9). God will lead the blind; he will not forsake his people. Those who trust in idols will be put to shame, and all creation will sing God's praise.
49:7-13	Kings who despise the Servant will prostrate themselves in response. God's people will be brought back from exile and returned to the Land of Promise. They will be comforted and cared for, led and provided for.
50:10-11	The Servant's word, received from God, is to be followed; it enables one to walk through darkness, trusting in God. Those who seek to provide their own "light" (i.e., who value their own direction over God's) will end in torment.
54:1-17	Instead of barrenness, there wll be renewed life and an end to reproach. The LORD has called his people back like a lost love—like Hosea does with his unfaithful wife. God reconfirms his steadfast love and eternal covenant of peace. He rebuilds the afflicted one and establishes her in beauty, righteousness, justice, and safety.

7. *Reading these Servant Songs in the bright light of the Cross, it is not hard to see the face of Christ. Yet, like many prophecies, they have both an immediate and a future fulfillment. We will look first at the temporal restoration promised to Judah and the immediate "servant" God sends to perform it.*

   a. *In Isaiah 43, God promises to overthrow Babylon, free his people, and restore them to their land. He then names the person who will enable them to return in Isaiah 44:28. What is his name, and what specific task will he be given?*

   A man named Cyrus, who God calls "my shepherd," is instrumental in God's plan. He will allow the people the freedom to go back to Jerusalem and rebuild the Temple.

   b. *Read* ***Isaiah 45:1-7.*** *For whose sake will God help this pagan ruler overthrow Babylon, and for what purpose?*

   God uses Cyrus to overthrow the nation that destroyed Jerusalem and exiled his people. It is for the sake of Israel and God's plan of redemption for all humanity that God calls Cyrus, strengthens him, and gives him success.

8. ***New Testament Connection:*** *As wonderful as the hope of a political redemption through Cyrus must have been, Isaiah gives a much more profound hope—of a spiritual Redeemer who will free all people from the grip of sin by taking on the punishment due them. Who is the "real," or ultimate, Redeemer-Servant to whom Cyrus points? Read* ***Acts 8:30-38.***

   a. *What part of Isaiah is quoted here?* Isaiah 53:7-8

   b. *How does Philip interpret this passage?*

   Beginning with the verse about the sheep led to slaughter, Philip explains how Isaiah is predicting the Good News of Jesus Christ. He is the Servant of whom Isaiah speaks.

   c. *Read* ***Isaiah 53:4-7.*** *How are some of the details fulfilled in Jesus Christ, according to the following New Testament verses? Make a note of which verses in Isaiah 53 provided your answers.*

   Matthew 27:12-14: Jesus remains silent when accused before the high priest (see Isaiah 53:7).

   John 1:29: Jesus is the Lamb of God who takes away the sins of the world (see Isaiah 53:6-7).

   1 Peter 2:23-25: Jesus does not retaliate when he is abused unjustly (see Isaiah 53:7); he bears our sins on the Cross (see Isaiah 53:5); we are like sheep gone astray (see Isaiah 53:6) but have returned to the true Shepherd.

   Romans 5:8: While we were sinners, Christ died for us (sec Isaiah 53:4-6).

"Arise, Shine; for Your Light Has Come": Zion Restored (Isaiah 56–66)

9. *Earlier we saw the figures of Cyrus and of the Servant, chosen and sent to redeem.*

   a. *Now read* ***Isaiah 59:15b-21,*** *and describe the messianic figure pictured there. What is his mission?*

   God is pictured as a divine warrior coming to intervene with justice and victory over his enemies. He is clothed in righteousness, salvation, vengeance, and fury, repaying his adversaries "according to their deeds" (59:18).

b. Read ***Isaiah 61:1-7.*** *What additional details does this tell us about the mission of the Lord's coming Anointed One?*

God's spirit is on the Messiah to bring news not only of vengeance on God's enemies, but the Good News ("gospel") of healing, freedom, comfort, and gladness to those who mourn and are in captivity. Their city will be built up, and they will be called priests and ministers of God.

Facilitators: Note that in Luke 4:16-21, Jesus launches his public ministry by quoting this passage from Isaiah as being fulfilled by himself. If you have time, read it and think about how Jesus fulfills this prophecy.

10. *Read* ***Isaiah 65:17-25.*** *Based on this passage, how would you describe the promised new creation, the New Jerusalem?*

    The New Jerusalem will be so glorious that it will completely eclipses any recollection of the old. It will be completely renewed and full of joy, with no sorrow or death. Justice and peace shall reign, and the hallmark of life will be joy, fulfillment, and blessing.

11. ***New Testament Connection:*** *Read* ***Revelation 21:1-5,*** *in which John is given a vision of a new heaven and new earth and of the arrival of the New Jerusalem. How does John's vision fulfill Isaiah's prophecy?*

    Isaiah foretells a new creation filled with joy and God's presence. John has a vision of this new creation and is told that it is where God will be present, living with his people. The old creation will be gone, just as Isaiah foresaw. This is the "new thing" Isaiah spoke of so long ago, a time when there would be no more death, sorrow, or pain.

D. Application

Facilitators: If time allows, have group members share their responses to the following application question.

Do you ever feel like you are away from God, like you cannot feel his presence? Do you ever feel forsaken or desolate? Review your notes about the Servant Songs and commentaries (questions 5 and 6). Choose the one that means the most to you and read it again. What consolation does it offer?

After the small-group discussion, watch Thomas Smith's video presentation on *Session 5* – Isaiah Part 2: Prophet of Consolation.

Session 6 – Responses

Jeremiah – The Broken-Hearted Prophet

Facilitators: *Read these recommended responses to the questions ahead of time to help you prepare to lead the small-group discussion.*

Participants: *Reinforce what you have learned by reviewing these recommended responses after the small-group discussion and before you continue to the next session.*

A. Establish the Context

Facilitators: Take a moment to establish the context and what was learned in the previous session.

B. Read the Story

Facilitators: If there is time, have someone read each passage aloud before it is discussed.

C. Take a Deeper Look

Kings of Judah in the Time of Jeremiah (2 Kings 22–24)

1. *It has been nearly a century since Israel's fall to Assyria, and Samaria is under foreign control. Jeremiah preaches to Judah, the Southern Kingdom, during the reigns of kings Josiah, Jehoiakim, and Zedekiah. Locate them on your* Bible Timeline *Chart; then read the following and record briefly what you learn about their reigns.*

    a. *Josiah – Judah's last faithful king*

    2 Kings 22:1-2: Josiah becomes king at the age of eight. He is a good king, doing "what was right in the eyes of the LORD, and walked in all the way of David his father." (You will notice that as their reigns are described, good kings are compared to King David, while others are said to have followed in the sins of Jeroboam.)

    2 Kings 23:1-5, 21-30 *(after Josiah has the Temple repaired and the Book of the Law is found in it):* Josiah has the words of the Law[1] read before all the people and renews the covenant between them and the LORD. He removes the pagan priests appointed by his predecessors, along with every vestige of idolatry in the land. He is praised for turning to God with his entire heart, soul, and strength in accordance with the Law of Moses. Josiah is slain on the battlefield, so he is spared the sight of God's punishment on Judah and Jerusalem (foretold in verses 26-27).

    b. *Jehoiakim*

    2 Kings 23:34-37: Jehoahaz does not follow Josiah but does evil in the sight of the LORD. Pharaoh Neco captures him, removes him to Egypt, and installs his brother Jehoiakim as king in his place. Jehoiakim is forced to pay tribute to Egypt, for which he taxes the people of Judah.

    2 Kings 24:1-2: When Babylon later invades the land, Jehoiakim becomes Nebuchadnezzar's vassal and rebels, after which Judah is invaded by marauding bands from neighboring kingdoms.

---

1 NAB: "book of the covenant" – likely the book of Deuteronomy, which records the terms of the second covenant under Moses, made with Israel on the plains of Moab before they entered the land of Canaan. In it, Moses explains how the people are to live in faithfulness to God and his commands.

c. *Zedekiah*

2 Kings 24:17–25:12: Mattaniah is made king by Babylon in his nephew's place, and his name is changed to Zedekiah. Like his immediate predecessors, he does evil in the sight of the LORD. This causes the LORD to cast him out of his presence. Zedekiah rebels against Babylon, so Nebuchadnezzar lays siege to Jerusalem. He kills Zedekiah's sons before his eyes, blinds him, and leads him bound in chains to Babylon. Nebuchadnezzar burns down Jerusalem and the Temple, taking the majority of Judah into exile, leaving only the poorest behind.

Jeremiah's Call and Message (Jeremiah 1–2)

2. *Chapter 1 tells how Jeremiah is called to be a prophet. Read* ***Jeremiah 1:1-5.***

a. *What four things does God tell Jeremiah about his calling?*

God formed Jeremiah in the womb; knew him before he created him; set him apart for a particular purpose even before he was born; and appointed him to be a prophet to the nations.

b. *Compare this to* ***Isaiah 44:1-2 and 49:1-6*** *(the call of the servant) and* ***Galatians 1:15-16*** *(the call of St. Paul). What do they have in common?*

The Servant and St. Paul, like Jeremiah, are called from the womb for a specific purpose—to speak God's Word to his people and, ultimately, to the nations.

3. *Read* ***Jeremiah 1:7-9.*** *Jeremiah's initial response is to object on the basis of his youth and ignorance. How does God reply?*

God tells Jeremiah not to be afraid but to go where he directs him and say what he commands. God promises to be with him and rescue him. He then touches Jeremiah's mouth, signifying that he has given him the very words he will ask him to speak.

4. *In* ***Jeremiah 1:10, 15-19,*** *God outlines Jeremiah's job description and the challenges he will face. What are the two opposite aspects of his role, and how will God help him accomplish them?*

Jeremiah is a prophet of both doom and restoration. His message is that God will uproot, break down, destroy, and overthrow—so that he can build and plant. Because Judah has forsaken the LORD, the time for judgment is upon them. Jeremiah's task is to announce this judgment. His message—to accept the consequences of their disobedience and submit to Babylon, so they will be spared—is not popular. The people and leaders of the land fight against Jeremiah; yet, God strengthens him like a fortified city and delivers him.

5. *In the following passages, what does Jeremiah's response in prayer to difficult circumstances reveal about the struggle within his heart?*

Jeremiah 17:14-18: Jeremiah expresses his trust in God, calling on him to be just and to protect and preserve him. In the midst of his suffering, he praises God. He asks the LORD to shore him up and not let terror or shame consume him.

Jeremiah 20:7-18: Jeremiah feels deceived, and in prayer, he is "honest to God." He reflects on the consequences of being a prophet (i.e., rejection), but he acknowledges that God's Word is greater than his will, which wants to shrink from the task. Even his own friends have turned against him. But his prayer ends with a confession of trust or praise: Yet, he trusts and praises God (verses 11-13).

6. *In Jeremiah 2, the prophet is called to plead for repentance in the streets of Jerusalem.*

   a. *Read* ***2:9-13.*** *What are the two great evils that Judah is charged with? Explain the metaphor Jeremiah uses to make them clear.*

   The people of Judah have committed two evils—they have forsaken God, and they have turned to other gods instead. Jeremiah illustrates the nature of this evil by contrasting a fountain of living waters (the LORD) with broken cisterns (pagan gods). A cistern is a waterproof receptacle for catching and holding rainwater. It is normally dug into the ground and lined to keep any of the water from seeping out. A broken cistern might catch the rain, but it would be unable to hold it, rendering it useless. In contrast, a fountain, with its continual source of fresh water, can overflow to the refreshment of all. In the presence of a fountain, no cistern is needed. It is thus shocking that the people would abandon a flowing fountain and build broken cisterns instead.

Facilitators: If there is time, ask someone to read John 4:7-15. Here, too, the water from a cistern is contrasted to living water. The people may have forsaken God, but here, his Son offers the living water of the Holy Spirit, which "wells up" to eternal life.

   b. *What are some of the leaky, inadequate "cisterns" we try to use to replace God in our lives?*

   Answers will vary; encourage discussion.

Jeremiah in the Temple

7. *Read* ***Jeremiah 7.***

   a. *What are some of the sins of Judah that are outlined here?*

   The people of Judah trust in the presence of the Temple while ignoring God's Law. Oppression and sin are rampant. They are disobedient and stubborn, refusing to listen and rejecting God's instruction and discipline. They even sacrifice their children in the fire of pagan altars.

   b. *The people of Judah may think Israel is destroyed only because it lacks the protection of the Temple. What historical event does Jeremiah recall to illustrate the folly of their belief? (See* ***verses 12-15.****)*

   Jeremiah reminds the people that Shiloh, the place the LORD first dwelt in the tabernacle after the conquest of Canaan (see Joshua 18:1), is no longer home to his presence (see Psalm 78:56-64). Not only has the tabernacle subsequently been moved, the entire Northern Kingdom of Israel (called "Ephraim" in verse 15) has been destroyed by Assyria. Given this history, the people should not harbor the false hope that the Temple—and, by extension, Judah—is immune to destruction.

8. ***New Testament Connection:*** *Read* ***Matthew 21:12-13,*** *where Jesus quotes both Isaiah 56:7 and Jeremiah 7:11. How does the context of the quote from Jeremiah give deeper meaning to Jesus' words? (Read also* ***CCC 584.****)*

   For Jesus, the Temple is a house of prayer, "the privileged place of encounter with God" (CCC 584). Some in Jesus' day have forgotten this and have begun using the Temple as a place of commerce. Jesus' allusion to Jeremiah 7:11 brings to mind the entire context: The people of Jeremiah's day blithely overlook the true purpose of the Temple, using it as a "good-luck charm" rather than a place of encounter with the one true God. They believe its very presence is a safeguard against their destruction. Lulled by this false hope, they continue in blatant sin and disregard for both God and his Law. In Jesus' day, everyone who hears him knows the outcome of that story: Not only Solomon's

Temple but all of Jerusalem has been destroyed. (A similar fate is in store for the rebuilt Temple and Jerusalem in AD 70.)

A Future and a Hope (Jeremiah 29–33)

9. *During this time, false prophets fill the air with claims that the exiles will be home soon from Babylon and all will be well. God sends a different message to the exiles through Jeremiah. Read **Jeremiah 29:1-14** before going on. (In the RSV-CE, "Jeconiah" in verse 2 is another name for Jehoiachin.)*

   a. *How are the exiles to live? Why? (See **verses 4-9.**)*

   Rather than listening to the false prophets who say they will soon return home, the exiles are told to settle in and establish themselves in Babylon: build homes, plant, marry, and have children. They are told to pray to the LORD on behalf of Babylon and that, as it prospers, so will they. They can do this because this is part of God's plan; they are not simply suffering the whims of a foreign invader.

   b. *The "why" of God's instructions becomes clearer in verses 10-14. What hope does he give them?*

   Picking up on what was only hinted at in verse 4 (i.e., that God is behind this move), God reminds Judah that his punishments are not capricious but are part of a long-term plan. There is a future and a hope awaiting the exiles: *good* plans for their future, not plans to do them harm. Their exile will be long but temporary. In seventy years, God will fulfill his promise and bring them back to their land. Absence, as the saying goes, will make their hearts grow fonder. They will then seek him and call upon him—things they were not doing in Judah before their exile—and they will find him. He will gather them from all the places to which they have been exiled, restore their fortunes, and bring them home.[2]

10. *Like Isaiah, Jeremiah has a "Book of Consolation." Chapters 30–33 are the "heart" of Jeremiah, full of beautiful words of restoration and hope, speaking of future days alluded to in Jeremiah's call—when, after uprooting and breaking down, God will watch over, build, and plant his people once again (see **1:10 and 31:28**).*

    *God is faithful to his covenant promise, but how can God be faithful given that his people have broken the covenant? Read **Jeremiah 31:31-37.***

   a. *Explain what God will do for his people (verses 31-34).*

   The LORD will make a New Covenant with not just Judah, but Israel as well (i.e., with his Chosen People as a whole). Though they broke the covenant he made with them through Moses at Sinai, he will forgive them and "remember their sins no more" (verse 34). In this New Covenant, instead of writing his Law on tablets of stone, he will write his law on their hearts. Everyone shall know him personally. (Recall what we discussed about the significance of the word "know" in Session 2 on Hosea.

   b. *How sure is this promise (verses 35-37)?*

   God's promise to Israel to make them his own is as sure as the order and extent of the universe—that is, endless and absolute.

---

2 Actually, not all of the exiles return to Judah. Thus, the return from Babylonian exile can be seen as symbolically foreshadowing the future "return" from the exile of sin that the Messiah, Jesus, will bring about.

11. *This promised "New Covenant" is something truly new. No amount of animal blood can atone for the sins of Israel. The breaking of the covenant requires the death of one of the parties. In God's mercy, he will send his own Son to take on Israel's sins—to become Israel, the Suffering Servant of Isaiah, in order to atone for its sins.*[3]

    Read the following passages, and explain what you learn about this "New Covenant" foretold by Jeremiah.

    Luke 22:19-20: The sign of the "New Covenant" is the Body and Blood of Christ in the Eucharist.

    CCC 781: The covenant God made with Israel was merely a preparation for the perfect covenant that will be established in Jesus, a covenant that will form not just a nation but "a people who might acknowledge him and serve him in holiness."[4] That people will transcend the family of Jacob and be made up of Jews and Gentiles both, united in Spirit.

    CCC 613: The New Covenant is ratified by the sacrifice of Christ's death, which reconciles to God a people separated from him by sin.

    CCC 1965: The New Covenant law, which is "the interior law of charity," is written on our hearts by the Holy Spirit.

D. Application

Facilitators: If time allows, have group members share their responses to the following application question.

We have seen into Jeremiah's heart in the way he prays in the midst of difficult and confusing circumstances. What about God's designs do you find hard to understand? Is there something you are going through that you think is difficult to bring to God in prayer? Choose one of Jeremiah's prayers from question 5. Rewrite it below to fit your situation, and offer it up to the Father.

After the small-group discussion, watch Thomas Smith's video presentation on *Session 6* – Jeremiah: The Broken-Hearted Prophet.

---

[3] See Romans 9:15-22.

[4] *Lumen Gentium* 9; see Acts 10:35; 1 Corinthians 11:25.

Session 7 – Responses
Ezekiel – God's Watchman on the Wall

Facilitators: *Read these recommended responses to the questions ahead of time to help you prepare to lead the small-group discussion.*

Participants: *Reinforce what you have learned by reviewing these recommended responses after the small-group discussion and before you continue to the next session.*

A. Establish the Context

Facilitators: Take a moment to establish the context and what was learned in the previous session.

B. Read the Story

Facilitators: If there is time, have someone read each passage aloud before it is discussed.

C. Take a Deeper Look

Ezekiel's Call and Ministry (Ezekiel 1–3)

1. *Read* ***Ezekiel 1.*** *Here, the prophet describes how the Word of the* L*ORD* *came to him in a strange and glorious vision. This is not an easy read. Even the great Church Father and Scripture scholar St. Jerome found Ezekiel to be a puzzle. Try not to get caught up in the details of the vision; simply read for the general sense of it.*

   a. *Where is Ezekiel? Where is the throne in Ezekiel's vision?*

   Ezekiel is with his fellow exiles by the River Chebar in Babylon. In his vision, the heavens are opened, and he sees a throne above him, apparently brought there by the wind on the backs of four winged creatures and a dazzling wheeled chariot with rims filled with eyes.

   b. ***Think About It:*** *What is the significance of this, as compared to the location of the throne in Isaiah's vision? (See* ***Isaiah 6:1-4*** *and "Establish the Context" on page 59.)*

   In Isaiah's vision, God's throne is in the Temple—which is not surprising, since God made the Temple his dwelling place and the Ark of the Covenant his throne. The people, however, believe that God's presence is *only* in Jerusalem (i.e., that God is contained there somehow in the land of Israel). Here they are, exiled, away from his presence. Now, in Ezekiel's vision, God's glory visits them in a foreign city in Babylon.

2. a. *Given the charge brought by several of the prophets that the people do not know the* L*ORD*, *this vision may be as important for the people to read as it is for Ezekiel to witness. What might they learn about God from Ezekiel 1?*

   This vision reveals God's glory and power in living color. Far from being made of wood like the idols the people worship, God's glory defies description. He is beyond creation, gloriously alive and beyond control. The people may think they have lost their God in exile—yet, here is God's glory, not tied to the Temple, but seeking out Ezekiel in enemy territory. The appearance of God's glory is so powerful that Ezekiel falls on his face in awe.

b. ***Think About It:*** *Today it might be hard to imagine God as tied to a particular physical country. But do we perhaps live as though he is confined to our churches? Comment on this. What application does Ezekiel 1 have for you?*

Answers will vary. Encourage discussion.

3. *Read* ***Ezekiel 2:1–3:11,*** *in which the Spirit enters Ezekiel and commissions him to speak on his behalf to "a nation of rebels" (2:3), "impudent and stubborn" (2:4); a rebellious house who may well refuse to listen to him. What is the scroll he is given, and what is the significance of having Ezekiel eat it?*

The scroll is the message God has for Israel, "words of lamentation and mourning and woe" (2:10). It is the words Ezekiel is to proclaim to the people. By eating the scroll, he will internalize God's words. They will be the LORD's words that he speaks, not his own. Interestingly, although the words are bitter, obedience (eating the scroll) is sweet.

4. *Read* ***Ezekiel 3:12-21.*** *What does it mean that God makes Ezekiel a "watchman" (verse 17) for the house of Israel? How critical is it for him to do his job?*

Like a watchman on a wall, Ezekiel is to watch and listen and alert the people when God sends warnings to them. The job, like that of a watchman, is crucial to their survival. If the people die without warning, the fault is his. If they do not listen to his warning and die, the fault is their own. And if they are warned and listen and turn from their sin, they will live because the watchman has saved their lives by his warning.

Judgment on Jerusalem (Ezekiel 4–24)

5. *The prophets speak of a "day of the LORD"[1]—not a single day, but a final day of reckoning, when God's glory and power will be revealed. Read* ***Ezekiel 7:2-3, 5-7, 10, 12-13.*** *What "has come" to Jerusalem?*

The same thing is described in a number of ways as having come: "the end," "your doom," "the time," "the day," "a day of tumult." The inescapable end to which all their actions have been heading has arrived. It is payday for Jerusalem (for those who refuse to turn their hearts to God).

6. a. *One year and one month after the chariot vision (592 BC, five years before the fall of Jerusalem) Ezekiel is transported to Jerusalem in a vision and shown terrible atrocities: idols standing in the Temple itself; elders, convinced the LORD does not see them, burning incense to idols there; and men with their backs to the Temple (the ultimate insult), worshiping the sun toward the east (Chapter 8). God calls on six divine "executioners" in Chapter 9 to deliver his wrath to the city. Before sending them to do their deadly work, what does God ask? (Read* ***Ezekiel 9:3-6.****)*

God calls on a man to mark the foreheads of all "who sigh and groan over all the abominations," and just as the angel of death passed over the Israelites who marked their doors with blood at the Exodus, these angels are to spare those with the marks on their foreheads from destruction.

Those people may not feel like they have been saved. They witness the carnage, and many are taken into exile—but along with the previous exiles, they are preserved as a "remnant." They are given a chance to recognize their distance from God and return to him spiritually. The exile may also feel like a punishment, but in fact it is a severe mercy, "tough love" from their heavenly Father. See Ezekiel 11:14-21 for God's words on this matter.

[1] See Isaiah 13:6, 9 and 58:13; Jeremiah 46:10; Ezekiel 13:5 and 30:3; Joel 1:15, 2:1, 11, 31, and 3:14; Amos 5:18, 20; Obadiah 1:15; Zephaniah 1:7, 8, 14; Zechariah 14:1; Malachi 4:5.

b. **Catechism *Connection:*** *Read* ***CCC 1296.*** *What do these Old Testament "marks" prefigure in the New Covenant today?*

Just as God asked the people to mark their doors during the Exodus, and as he marked those people who "groan over all the abominations" (9:4) during Ezekiel's time, God continues to mark the faithful as his own. Christians are marked with the seal of the Holy Spirit at baptism to show they belong to Christ. It also is a divine "seal of protection" for the trial to come at the end of time.

7. *In Chapter 10, wheeled cherubim like those in Chapter 1 appear over the court of the Temple. Read* ***Ezekiel 10:3-4, 10:18-19, and 11:22-23.*** *Trace the movement of the glory of the* Lord*, and comment on its significance.*

The glory of the Lord, enthroned on the cherubim, rises from the Temple and moves to the threshold of the inner court, then to the east gate, and finally leaves the city altogether and stands upon the mountain to the east of Jerusalem (the Mount of Olives). The sins of the people are so bad, and they have defiled the Temple to such an extent, that God's presence and holiness can remain there no longer.

Future Restoration (Ezekiel 33–48)

8. *Read* ***Ezekiel 34.***

a. *Who are the shepherds addressed in verses 1-10, and what charge does the* Lord *make against them?*

The shepherds are the leaders of Israel. Rather than caring for the people, they are living at their expense. They have not strengthened, healed, restored, or searched for those in need. Rather, they have ruled them harshly. As a result of corrupt shepherds, the people are scattered to the nations with no one to look after them.

b. *What will God do for his sheep, according to verses 11-16?*

God himself will seek out the scattered sheep, rescue them from the places to which they have been exiled, and bring them home to their own land. There, he himself will be their shepherd, provide for and care for them, give them rest, heal and strengthen them, and rule them justly.

c. *In verses 23-24, there is a transition from "I myself" (the shepherd in verse 15) to another who will shepherd the sheep. Who is it? Describe him.*

God will set up one shepherd over them—"my servant David"—who will feed and shepherd them on his behalf. Here is an echo of Isaiah's "Servant." David is the king God set over Israel in its early days, four hundred years previously. In his original covenant with David (2 Samuel 7), God promised to give him an everlasting throne over all of Israel.

9. ***New Testament Connection:*** *Read the following passages from John's Gospel and answer the questions.*

John 10:11-18: *How does Jesus resolve this dilemma between God and his "servant David" shepherding his sheep? (See also* ***CCC 754.****)*

Christ the Messiah ("Anointed One") is the anointed descendant of David who rules on the Davidic throne. As the second Person of the Trinity, he is also "God himself." As the *Catechism* points out, the Church is the flock nourished and led by Jesus. Jesus is the Good Shepherd referred to in Ezekiel. Unlike the "bad shepherds" (leaders of Israel) who care nothing for the sheep and fail to protect and care for them, he shepherds the people to the point of laying down his life for them.

***John 6:51-58:** If Jesus is the Good Shepherd described by Ezekiel, how does he feed his flock?*

Jesus provides the "living bread" of his own flesh and the "true drink" of his blood to nourish his sheep. Anyone who feeds on him will have eternal life because of him.

10. *God's restoration of Israel will go far beyond returning the people to the land. Their exile is a reflection of their self-imposed, internal "exile" from communion with God. A true return will need to be effected internally as well. Read **Ezekiel 36:22-27.** What does God promise, and why?*

    For the sake of his name, which they have profaned among the nations, God will restore them to their land. Not only that, he will cleanse them from their sins and idolatry and give them a new heart and spirit so they can walk in obedience as his people.

11. *Fourteen years after the conquest of Jerusalem, Ezekiel is granted a vision in which a future, restored Temple is revealed and measured.*

    a. *Read **Ezekiel 43:1-7.** What does he see, and what is he told?*

    Ezekiel sees the glory of the LORD entering the Temple by the east gate and filling the Temple. God's presence is with them again. Then he is told that this Temple is the place where God will dwell with and rule the people of Israel forever.

    b. *In Chapter 47, Ezekiel describes the life-giving, healing waters pouring forth from the Temple.[2] The renewed Temple will be at the heart of the renewed land of Israel and a renewed Jerusalem. What will be the name of the city? (See **48:35.**)*

    How fitting that Ezekiel's book closes with an admonition to call the renewed Jerusalem, "The LORD is there." At the center of all these covenant promises is a relationship with Yahweh. This ultimate covenant promise of God's eternal, intimate presence with his people, living among them, will be true to the point of characterizing the city—pre-figuring a time when God will live among us as the man Immanuel, "God with us."

12. *God's beautiful promise of a new, indwelling Spirit has been fulfilled at Pentecost, and all the baptized now receive this marvelous gift. Read **CCC 736 and 1432.** What about God's gift of a new heart and spirit, as explained here, particularly speaks to you, and why?*

    Answers will vary; encourage discussion.

D. Application

Facilitators: If time allows, have group members share their responses to the following application question.

Do you or your parish feel dry or lifeless like the dry bones in Ezekiel 37? Read that chapter again, and consider how you can you take hope from that vision and its revelation of the power of God.

After the small-group discussion, watch Thomas Smith's video presentation on *Session 7* – Ezekiel: God's Watchman on the Wall.

2 For further study, compare Ezekiel's Temple vision with John's vision of the New Jerusalem in Revelation 21-22, and see John's use of this imagery in John 7:37-39, 19:34.

Session 8 – Responses
Daniel – Faithful to the End

Facilitators: Read these recommended responses to the questions ahead of time to help you prepare to lead the small-group discussion.*

***Participants:** Reinforce what you have learned by reviewing these recommended responses after the small-group discussion and before you continue to the next session.*

A. Establish the Context

Facilitators: Take a moment to establish the context and what was learned in the previous session.

B. Read the Story

Facilitators: If there is time, have someone read each passage aloud before it is discussed.

C. Take a Deeper Look

Daniel in Nebuchadnezzar's Court (Daniel 1–6)

1. *Read* ***Daniel 1.*** *What kind of person is Daniel as a teenager?*

   Daniel is one of the most promising young men of Judea: a handsome, healthy member of the nobility; educated, wise, and competent enough to be desired by Nebuchadnezzar to serve in his court. Daniel's head is not turned by the special treatment he receives; rather, he is determined to remain undefiled by the rich food offered to him. (It is possible that this food from the king's kitchen was previously offered to idols, which would explain his refusal.) His dealings with the steward reveal prudence and courage, skill in negotiating, and trust in God's care. God has blessed him with skill and wisdom beyond all others in the kingdom, along with the ability to interpret dreams.

2. *Daniel and his companions are given new names, as noted in the chart on page 68.*

   Read ***CCC 203.*** *What is significant about the way these names are changed?*

   As the *Catechism* says, a name is more than a label; it expresses one's identity and the meaning of one's life. The boys had Hebrew names that incorporated a name of God (*-el* for "Elohim" or *-iah* for "Yahweh"), identifying them with the God of Israel. Now, in Babylon, their names reflect the names of foreign gods and assert their supposed allegiance to those gods.

3. *Read* ***Daniel 2:1-23,*** *in which Nebuchadnezzar poses a seemingly impossible question: not only "interpret my dream," but also, "what did I dream?"*

   a. *Learning that he is slated to die along with the wise men who cannot tell the dream, Daniel seeks an audience with the king. What does Daniel intend to do, and how does he prepare?*

      Daniel determines to provide the dream and interpretation to the king. The first thing he does after getting on the king's calendar is to gather his friends and pray—a fine measure of his faith.

   b. *What does Daniel's prayer in verses 21-23 reveal about his knowledge of God?*

Daniel knows God. He blesses God for his eminent wisdom and might; for his sovereignty over all kings; and for his provision of wisdom and understanding. God is the source of wisdom, strength, and knowledge; he knows things that are secret and is able to reveal mysteries. Above all this, perhaps, Daniel is confident in approaching God, who he is certain will come to his aid.

4. *Read* ***Daniel 2:24-49.***

   a. *Nebuchadnezzar dreamed of a mighty and frightening image: a statue with a head of gold, breast and arms of silver, belly and thighs of bronze, legs of iron, and feet of iron and clay. What happens in his dream as he looks upon this image? (See* ***verses 34-35.****)*

   As Nebuchadnezzar watches, a stone appears out of nowhere and hits the feet, breaking them into pieces. Destruction spreads up the rest of the image until the pieces are reduced to a powder and lost forever to the wind. Meanwhile, the stone grows to become a mountain that fills the earth.

   b. *What interpretation does God provide through Daniel to the king?*

   The image grants Nebuchadnezzar a view of the future: a succession of kingdoms beginning with his own mighty empire. At the end, in a time of instability represented by an iron and clay mixture, God will set up an everlasting "kingdom which shall never be destroyed."

5. *Read* ***Daniel 3.***[1] *Perhaps inspired by his dream, King Nebuchadnezzar builds an enormous golden image, sixty by six cubits (ninety by nine feet) in size. He orders everyone in the kingdom to bow before it or be cast into a furnace of fire. Daniel's compatriots, themselves in positions of prominence in the kingdom, refuse.*

   a. *Read the king's question and the men's answer in verses 14-18. What is really at stake in this trial? (See the end of* ***verse 15.****)*

   Nebuchadnezzar's question is unexpected. Not only "worship the statue … or be instantly cast into the white-hot furnace," but, "Who is the god that can deliver you out of my hands?" The lives of the men are at risk, but it is God's reputation and standing that is ultimately at stake. Who or what is most worthy of worship: the king, the state, this golden image, or the One who made them all? In support of their faith in the LORD, the men willingly put their lives in God's hands and leave the proof of the matter to him.

   b. *What happens to the men who refuse to bow to the image, and how do they respond to their punishment?*

   Nebuchadnezzar orders the furnace super-heated and the young men bound and thrown inside. The heat kills the men who carry them there but does not harm the captives. Azariah (Abednego) offers a penitential prayer and implores the LORD's mercy for the sake of his name. The fire is stoked higher but it only serves to kill the king's servants, while the angel of the LORD comes down with "a moist whistling wind" so the men in the fire are not touched—whereupon the three break out into a glorious hymn of praise.

   c. *How does Nebuchadnezzar respond?*

   Nebuchadnezzar is astonished at the sight of a fourth man, "like a son of the gods," in the fire and by seeing the men unharmed. In an ironic twist, he calls them out of the furnace by their Babylonian names but identifies them as "servants of the Most High God." He blesses the God

[1] Text note: The section of Daniel 3 containing the prayers of Azariah and his companions was composed in Hebrew or Aramaic but then translated into Greek and preserved in the Septuagint. It appears in Catholic (but not Protestant) Bibles. Verse numbering varies with the translation. The RSV-CE numbers its verses from 1-68 and sets the prayers off in italics between 3:23 and 3:24. [They are named as "song verses" in this lesson to avoid confusion; see 6a.] The NAB inserts the hymn directly into the text as verses 24-90 and re-numbers the remaining verses so they flow consecutively.

who has saved them and decrees that no one shall speak against him—"for there is no other god who is able to deliver in this way." Already positioned as leaders in Babylon, the men are given political promotions—a fitting rebuke to those who sought to destroy them (3:8ff).

6. *The remnant of Judah has been exiled to the epicenter of worldly power and wisdom. The very fact of their exile seems to argue against the power of the Lord. Yet, when the Lord shows him the king's dream, Daniel says, "Blessed be the name of God forever and ever, for wisdom and power are his" (2:20). In the midst of a furnace, which might stand for the plight of Israel, Azariah and the others echo Daniel's praise in a powerful hymn.*

   Read the Song in ***verses 28-68*** *aloud (NAB: 3:52-90).*[2]

   a. *What three categories of beings are called upon to praise and glorify God? For help with this question, see sections beginning with* ***verses 36, 52, and 60*** *(NAB: 3:58, 74, 82).*

      The men call on all creation to lift praise to God, beginning with the heavens and all within them (including angels and other powers; the sun, moon, and stars; and the elements and weather); then the earth and its creatures; and finally all people (verses 60-66; NAB: 3:82-88).

7. *Read* ***Daniel 6.*** *(Darius—"royal one"—is a Mede; he may have been a general appointed over Babylon, a governor with king-like powers.) What does Daniel's response to the king's decree show about the strength of his faith? (See* ***verse 10.****)*

   Not even the threat of death causes Daniel to change his spiritual habits or hide his habit of prayer. He kneels by the open window of his room and prays and thanks God where anyone can see him. His faith is such that he does not fear what man can do to him, but serves God regardless of threats.

Daniel's Visions (Daniel 7–12)

8. *Read* ***Daniel 7,*** *in which Daniel receives a vision of God's view of the coming kingdoms, one that parallels the vision Nebuchadnezzar received in Chapter 2.*

   a. *Fill in the empty boxes below to show how Daniel sees the kingdoms that Nebuchadnezzar sees as parts of a human image.*

World Empires[3]	Nebuchadnezzar's Vision (Daniel 2:32-33) A statue of a man	Daniel's Vision (Daniel 7:3-7, 20) Four beasts
1	Gold head	Lion with eagle's wings that stands like a man
2	Silver chest, arms	Bear with three ribs that devours much flesh
3	Bronze belly, thighs	Leopard with four wings, four heads that is given dominion
4	Iron legs; Clay and iron feet	Dreadful, strong beast with iron teeth, ten horns; small horn with eyes and mouth

[2] Does the song sound familiar? This well-loved prayer is part of the prayers of the Divine Office, featured in Morning Prayer as an Old Testament Canticle.

[3] The visions propose a succession of world empires leading up to the establishment and spread of the kingdom of God. The traditional interpretation is that these world empires are Babylon, Medo-Persia, Greece, and Rome. Other scholars identify them as Babylon, Media, Persia, and Greece (however, the Medes were never an empire on their own).

Facilitators: Note that Daniel says the empires look "like" these beasts, not that actual beasts will come on the earth. As is typical with apocalyptic literature, physical examples from life are used to represent spiritual truths. They are not intended to be interpreted literally.

b. *In Nebuchadnezzar's vision, a stone comes from nowhere and smashes the statue to nothing before growing to fill the earth. In Daniel's vision, God appears on a fiery throne and sits in judgment on the nations, destroying the last beast and taking away the dominion of the others. What does Daniel see next that corresponds to the stone in Daniel 2? (See* ***7:13-14.****)*

The kingdom-stone corresponds in Daniel's vision to the rule of "one like a son of man coming, on the clouds of heaven" (verse 13). God (the "Ancient One," verse 9) confers on him dominion over every people and nation, a rule that will never end and a kingdom that will never be destroyed.

c. ***New Testament Connection:*** *"Son of Man" is the title Jesus most often uses to refer to himself. Read the following verses and record what you learn about Jesus as Son of Man.*

Matthew 25:31-32: He will come in glory with the angels and sit on his throne to judge the nations.

Matthew 24:30: At the end of the age, he will come with the clouds in power and great glory and gather his elect.

Matthew 17:12, 22-23: He will suffer, die, and be raised.

9. *In Chapter 9, Daniel—who is now an old man—realizes that the seventy-year period of exile prophesied by Jeremiah is coming to an end.*[4] *He goes before God in sackcloth and ashes, confessing the sins of the people and begging for forgiveness on their behalf. Read* **Daniel 9:16-19.** *For what does Daniel plead, and on what basis?*

Daniel asks the LORD to turn his favor upon desolate Jerusalem—not on the basis of any good they have done, but because they and the city are called by God's name. They "have become a byword" among the surrounding nations (verse 16), reflecting badly upon the reputation of the LORD.

10. *As Daniel continues in prayer, the angel Gabriel comes to enlighten him with "wisdom and understanding" of the future, because of God's great love for him (9:22-23). What, in general, does Gabriel tell him in 9:24?*

The seventy years decreed for exile will not be the end, but "seventy weeks of years" (seventy times seven, or 490 years) remain before atonement, the end of the power of sin, and the arrival of everlasting righteousness. Whatever the meaning of those years, it is sufficient here to note that even as the physical exile comes to end, there is still work to be done for a full restoration of God's kingdom.

It is interesting to note that the next time Gabriel is mentioned in Scripture (in Luke 1), it is once again the time of the evening sacrifice. This time he is announcing the birth of John who is the "voice crying in the wilderness" prophesied in Isaiah 40. Three chapters later, Jesus launches his public ministry by proclaiming himself to be the liberating Messiah of Isaiah 61. The true return from the exile of sin has begun.

11. *Daniel is given further visions about the coming eras, in which the successive empires are the visible face of a battle in the heavens. In retrospect, we know that even after returning from exile, the Jews will live under a series of Gentile rulers for that 490-year period, which culminates at the time of Jesus Christ.*

[4] See Jeremiah 25:11, 29:10-14.

Read **Daniel 12:1-3.** *What hope is given to Daniel and, through him, to the people?*

The heavenly messenger assures Daniel that in spite of trouble the likes of which have never been seen before, the "great prince" (archangel) Michael has charge over God's people and will deliver them. Even those who die will rise again to everlasting life or everlasting contempt in the end.

This is the first and one of the clearest indications in Scripture of the future resurrection, which has been revealed gradually over time. To learn what the Church teaches about bodily resurrection, see Article 11 in the *Catechism,* especially paragraphs 992–1001.

D. Application

Facilitators: If time allows, have group members share their responses to the following application question.

Daniel and his companions stand out in the Old Testament as remarkable examples of faithful lives lived in the face of inconvenience, opposition, and persecution. A hymn called "Dare to Be a Daniel" used to be sung in their praise:

Standing by a purpose true,
Heeding God's command,
Honor them, the faithful few!
All hail to Daniel's band!

Refrain:

Dare to be a Daniel,
Dare to stand alone!
Dare to have a purpose firm!
Dare to make it known.

What inconveniences, opposition, or persecution do you face in your life that might prevent you from worshiping God? What have you learned from Daniel's life and visions that might help you "dare to be a Daniel"?

After the small-group discussion, watch Thomas Smith's video presentation on *Session 8* – Daniel: Faithful to the End.

Session 9 – Responses

Haggai and Malachi – Messengers of Hope

Facilitators: *Read these recommended responses to the questions ahead of time to help you prepare to lead the small-group discussion.*

Participants: *Reinforce what you have learned by reviewing these recommended responses after the small-group discussion and before you continue to the next session.*

A. Establish the Context

Facilitators: Take a moment to establish the context and what was learned in the previous session.

B. Read the Story

Facilitators: If there is time, have someone read each passage aloud before it is discussed.

C. Take a Deeper Look

HAGGAI

Historical Background from the Book of Ezra

1. *All three prophets of the Return should be read in the context of the historical background conveyed in the books of Ezra and Nehemiah. Ezra 1–6 tells of the first return (under Zerubbabel) and of the building of the Temple.*

   a. *Read* ***Ezra 1:1–2:2.*** *How does God bring about an end to the time of Babylonian exile?*

   God "[stirs] up the spirit" of the Persian king to allow the Jews to return to Jerusalem and rebuild his Temple. Cyrus returns the holy vessels removed from the Temple by Nebuchadnezzar and tells those who have not returned to assist the others by means of free-will offerings to support the building effort.

   b. *The people do not return to an empty land. Judea is now a province of Persia, administered from Samaria and populated by the unskilled, uneducated people the Babylonians have left behind. In the countryside to the north are the descendants of exiles from other lands (moved there by the Assyrians). These have mixed Israelite practices with the worship of other gods.*[1] *Read* ***Ezra 4.*** *Briefly describe how the returned exiles fare as they work to build the Temple.*

   The people of the land, "adversaries of Judah and Benjamin," discourage the returned exiles and work hard to frustrate their cause. They turn the authorities against them, stopping their work for more than fifteen years—into the time of King Darius of Persia (who reigns from 522–486 BC).

The Word of the Lord Comes by Haggai (Book of Haggai)

2. *Read* ***Haggai 1,*** *which describes the first "word" or message from God.*

   a. *The Temple has lain in ruins for decades. What have the people been doing? Where have they placed their priorities?*

---

[1] See 2 Kings 17:24-41.

The people have been working on their own houses, tending to their own comfort and pleasure instead of tending to the house of the LORD. Meanwhile, their own houses are "paneled" (verse 4). And they have "looked for much" (verse 9) by sowing, drinking, and earning money to fill themselves.

b. *Has focusing on their own priorities paid off for them? Explain (see **verses 5-6 and 9-11**).*

Focusing on their own priorities to the neglect of the LORD's has not paid off. The people may have houses, but their efforts to reap large harvests, build their bank accounts, and be successful have been "blown away" by God, who has withheld his blessing from them.

3. a. *Although they are back in the land, blessings do not automatically follow. Read about the covenant promises and curses God gives them through Moses in Deuteronomy 28:1-6 and 15-19. What do you learn?*

God's blessing—including his blessings on them, on their crops and their cattle, and on all their activities—is dependent on their obedience to God's covenant commandments.

b. *What is the solution to their struggle? (See also **Haggai 1:8.**)*

The solution is obedience to God's command to build his house. God wants to know they desire his presence among them. By abandoning the Temple, they have returned in body but not in spirit.

4. *Given the determined opposition the people face, one might be tempted to excuse them for letting the Temple go until a more opportune time. Read **1 Kings 6:11-13 and 8:41-43.** Why is it so important for the LORD to have a "house" in the world?*

God's "house" (the Temple) is the place where God promises to dwell with his covenant people. It is also to be a witness of his power to the Gentiles. By failing to rebuild it, the returned exiles not only rob themselves of a place of worship, they do not look like God's people in the eyes of the world, and they are not displaying God's glory for others to see and potentially turn to.

5. *Review **Haggai 1:12-14.** When Zerubbabel, Joshua, and the people respond in obedience, what message and concrete help does God give them? (See also **2:4-5.**)*

"I am with you, says the LORD" (verse 13). Imagine: Even without the Temple, he assures them of his presence. Then he "[stirs] up the spirit" (verse 14) of the leaders and the people so that they begin work on the Temple again. Three times in Chapter 2 God tells them to take courage or not to fear—because he is with them, his Spirit abiding among them.

6. *Ezra 3:10-12 describes how those who are old enough to remember the original Temple weep at the sight of the new foundation. Solomon had vast resources at his disposal, and the original Temple was glorious. It is obvious, even at this early stage of building, that the new structure is no match for the first. According to **Haggai 2:4-9,** should they be concerned? Why, or why not?*

No, the people should take courage because God's Spirit is with them. The time will come when God will cause the Temple to be filled with treasures from the world over, and he will fill it with his glory. Those who think it looks like "nothing" (verse 3) need not fear. "The latter splendor of this house shall be greater than the former, says the LORD of hosts" (verse 9), and they will prosper.

7. *The theme of "considering" runs through Haggai. In just two chapters, the people are asked three times to consider how they have fared as they have pursued their own priorities to no avail—because they have*

failed to return to God (1:5, 7, 2:15, 18). Read those verses and ***Haggai 2:18-20.*** *What encouraging thing should they "consider from this day onward"?*

From this day onward, God says, even though until now their efforts have not borne fruit, "I will bless you." Haggai is a messenger of hope.

MALACHI

Historical Background from the Books of Ezra and Nehemiah

8. *Read* ***Nehemiah 13:4-31,*** *which describes the state of Judea when Nehemiah returns after an absence. Describe briefly the four things Nehemiah finds that trouble him.*

   Nehemiah finds that (1) the courts of the Temple are being used for lodgings, (2) the tithes are being mismanaged, with the result that the Levites and singers are no longer in service in the Temple for they have not been provided for as the Law requires, (3) the Sabbath is being profaned by people carrying burdens and carrying on business within Jerusalem, and (4) some of the people are marrying foreign wives.

The Word of the Lord Comes by Malachi (Book of Malachi)

9. *"I have loved you," says the Lord in Malachi 1:2. Yet the people do not see it. They are blinded by their own sins. Read the following verses and note the ways the covenant is broken.*

Malachi	Covenant Broken	Breaches of the Covenant
2:1-9	The covenant of Levi, "a covenant of life and peace" (verse 5)	The priests have failed to give glory to God's name (verse 2). Instead of teaching truth and walking uprightly, they have turned from the way and have led others astray also.
2:10-11	"The covenant of our fathers" (verse 10)	"Judah" and "Jacob" (these names of two of the "fathers" refer here to the nation that sprang from them) have been unfaithful to their heavenly Father, to the God who covenanted with Abraham, Isaac, and Jacob before them to make them a nation of his own. Specifically, they have married foreign wives (people who worship false gods), which is against the covenant.
2:14-16	The covenant of marriage ("between you and the wife of your youth," verse 14)	They are being faithless to their wives, divorcing them.

10. *In* ***Malachi 2:17,*** *we read that the people protest this characterization of themselves. They wonder how it can matter whether they follow the Law, when it seems as though lawbreakers get away with wrong and are blessed by the Lord.*

    a. *To those who believe God does not act when his Law is broken, Malachi announces in 3:2 "the day of his coming" in judgment, but asks, "who can endure" that day? Read the following passages and tell what that day will bring.*

Malachi 3:1-5: The LORD will come to his Temple suddenly (verse 1), coming near them "for judgment" (verse 5). He will come "like a refiner's fire" (verse 2) to purify the Levites so that righteous, acceptable offerings will once again be brought to him. Then he will judge those who have broken their marriage covenants, their bonds of trust and friendship, and those who cheat and oppress the weak and needy and do not fear him.

Malachi 4:1: That day will come "burning like an oven," turning to stubble and setting on fire all the proud and those who do evil.

b. *In light of God's coming in fiery judgment on that day, is there hope for anyone? Read* ***Malachi 3:6-7****, and record what you learn.*

The LORD assures them that he does not change, which is why some of them remain and have not been destroyed even after repeatedly breaking his covenant. The same LORD who covenanted with their fathers is there for them now—if they will only return to him.

11. *Malachi 3 and 4 speak of someone who will come just prior to the day of the LORD. What do the following verses tell you about this person and his purpose?*

Verses in Malachi	Person and Description	Purpose
3:1	God's messenger	The LORD will send him to prepare the way before him.
4:5-6 *(NAB or New Jerusalem: 3:23-24)*	"Elijah the prophet"	God will send him ahead to prepare God's people for his coming by turning the hearts of the fathers to their children and vice versa. The goal of his coming is to prepare people that they might be spared judgment, which will fall as a curse on those who do not turn.

12. *Now read* ***Malachi 4:1-6*** *(NAB and New Jerusalem: Malachi 3:19-24).*

a. *While "all the arrogant and all evildoers" will be as though burned to stubble at the day of the LORD, what can be expected by those who fear the LORD?*

Rather than burning them, the fire of that day will be a healing fire; those who fear God will "go forth leaping" like calves newly released from the stall, and the wicked will be like nothing but ashes beneath their feet.

b. *Compare* ***verses 5-6*** *(NAB: 3:23-24) with* ***Luke 1:17,*** *which is part of the angel Gabriel's message to Zechariah. (For context, read* ***Luke 1:8-17.****) What interpretation does the angel give to Malachi's prophecy?*

The child born to Zechariah and Elizabeth, John the Baptist, will be the messenger spoken of in Malachi. He will "go before [the LORD] in the spirit and power of Elijah, to turn the hearts of the fathers to the children" (Luke 1:17) and prepare the people for the coming of the Lord Jesus Christ.

13. *Read **James 4:6-9.** What does this add to your understanding of God's love and judgment and how we can approach him, even now?*

    Answers will vary. God may oppose the proud, yet he gives abundant grace to the humble. His love is greater than any sin. Those who submit to God and resist the devil will find that the devil flees along with his temptations. "Draw near to God and he will draw near to you" calls to mind Malachi 3:7: "Return to me, and I will return to you." The way to draw near is to turn from sin, cleanse your hands, and purify your heart. Sorrow and dejection will be turned around as God exalts those who humble themselves before him.

D. Application

Facilitators: If time allows, have group members share their responses to the following application question.

In our time, Pope Francis has renewed the call from Jesus, originally heard by St. Francis of Assisi, to "rebuild my Church." What spiritual building projects does the Church face today? What are the challenges? How are you participating?

After the small-group discussion, watch Thomas Smith's video presentation on *Session 9* – Haggai and Malachi: Messengers of Hope.

New Testament and Modern Prophets – Messengers of the New Covenant

Facilitators: Read these recommended responses to the questions ahead of time to help you prepare to lead the small-group discussion.

Participants: Reinforce what you have learned by reviewing these recommended responses after the small-group discussion.

A. Establish the Context

Facilitators: Take a moment to establish the context and what was learned in the previous session.

B. Read the Story

Facilitators: If there is time, have someone read each passage aloud before it is discussed.

C. Take a Deeper Look

The Long-Expected Prophet Comes

1. *John the Baptist fulfills the prophecy in Isaiah 40 of one who will come to prepare the way of the Lord. Read* ***Luke 3:1-18.***

   a. *What does John do to prepare the way for Jesus?*

   John the Baptist prepares the way for Christ by preaching a baptism of repentance for the forgiveness of sins (healing the ruptured relationship between God and his people). It is a preparatory cleansing for the people to welcome Christ.

   b. *How is his message like that of the Old Testament prophets?*

   Like that of the Old Testament prophets, John the Baptist's message is one that calls people to "bear fruits that befit repentance" (3:8) and that exposes their false trust in their ethnic heritage alone as the way to please God. When they insist that, "We have Abraham as our father," their attitude is not unlike that of the people who put false trust in the Temple in the time of Jeremiah (Jeremiah 7). In Luke 3:9, John warns the people of a coming judgment if they do not return to the Lord. The imagery of a tree, root and branch, being thrown into the fire reminds us of the fiery language of Malachi (Malachi 3:1-4, 4:1-2). John is also like the Old Testament prophets in pointing out the problem of corruption and violence (Isaiah 1:21-23).

2. *If John the Baptist is the messenger or forerunner announced by Malachi, Jesus is the One whose coming he announces.*[1] *Matthew purposefully draws attention to events in Jesus' life that fulfill messianic prophecies. Choose four or more of the following passages and tell how Jesus fulfills the prophecies that are quoted in them. The Old Testament references are provided for your information.*

   Matthew 1:18-23 *(Isaiah 7:14 and 8:8, 10):* A virgin shall conceive and bear a son called Emmanuel (God with us): Mary, a virgin, conceives a son who is truly God with us.

[1] See Matthew 3:11-12; Mark 1:1-11; Luke 3:1-22; John 1:19-34.

Matthew 2:1-6 *(Micah 5:2):* From Bethlehem will come a ruler who will govern Israel: Jesus is born in Bethlehem and recognized by wise men as king of the Jews.

Matthew 2:13-15 *(Hosea 11:1):* God's "Son" will be called out of Egypt (an event foreshadowed when Israel, who God called his "firstborn," is brought out of Egypt in the Exodus): Joseph takes Mary and the infant Jesus to Egypt until the death of Herod.

Matthew 4:12-16 *(Isaiah 9:1-2, 42:7; Amos 5:8):* "A great light" will dawn from Zebulun and Naphtali on those who sit in darkness: After being tempted by the devil (4:1-11), Jesus (the light of the world) withdraws into Galilee and begins his ministry from the territory of Zebulun and Naphtali.

Matthew 8:14-17 *(Isaiah 53:4):* The Messiah will take on our infirmities and bear our diseases: Jesus heals many who were sick and casts out many demons.

Matthew 13:34-35 *(Psalm 78:2):*[2] The Messiah will speak hidden things in parables: Jesus speaks to the crowds in parables.

Matthew 21:1-5 *(Zechariah 9:9):* Zion's king will come humbly, riding on an ass, and on a colt: Jesus sends his disciples to bring him an ass and a colt to ride into Jerusalem on.

3. *Not only does Jesus fulfill messianic prophecy, he also is the "ultimate" prophet.*

   a. *Read* **Deuteronomy 18:15, 18-19,** *and describe what was promised more than one thousand years before the birth of Christ.*

   God promised to raise up a prophet like Moses from among the people of Israel, who the people shall "heed" (listen to and obey). God will put his words into his mouth, and he shall speak what God commands him.

   b. *Read the following verses and comment on who recognizes Jesus as that prophet, and why. (You may want to start a few verses ahead of each passage to get the context.)*

   John 6:14: After the miracle of the loaves and fishes (when Jesus feeds the people like Moses fed with manna), the people recognize Jesus as "the prophet who is to come into the world."

   Acts 3:20-26: Peter, after healing the lame man, tells the people that the prophet foretold by Moses, appointed for them and the one they should listen to, is Jesus Christ.

   John 8:26, 28: Jesus teaches the Jews that the things he says, he has received from the Father and not on his own authority. (The expected prophet was to speak only the words God put into his mouth.)

4. *Now read* **Hebrews 1:1-3 and 2:1-3.** *In what way is Jesus a prophet in an even deeper sense than the Old Testament prophets were?*

   God speaks through the Old Testament prophets, but in Jesus Christ, his Word actually becomes flesh. Hebrews 1:1 speaks of him as a kind of "final word" spoken after the long line of Old Testament prophets. Because Jesus "reflects the glory of God and bears the very stamp of his nature" (verse 3), he perfectly reflects that Word into the world with the power that upholds the universe. The author of Hebrews points out at the start of Chapter 2 that in light of who Jesus is, "we must pay the closer attention to what we have heard." This brings to mind the prophecy of the

[2] Psalm 78 is attributed to Asaph, who is called a prophet in 2 Chronicles 29:30 (LXX).

prophet like Moses, who the people are to "heed." Even more so must they heed the very Word of God, sent by God.

5. *The renowned Jewish scholar Abraham Heschel wrote that the prophet is "one who bears testimony to God's concern for human beings. ... His fundamental objective was to reconcile man and God."*[3] ***Think About It:*** *How does Jesus exemplify this in a most perfect manner? (For help with this question, read* ***John 3:16*** *and* ***Colossians 1:19-20.****)*

   Answers will vary. Jesus bears testimony to God's concern for human beings in the deepest way possible not just by warnings and promises, but by taking their humanity and sin upon himself. By dying on the Cross he restores them to a right and life-giving relationship with the Father. Jesus is the Suffering Servant foretold by Isaiah. We are reconciled to God by the blood of the Cross.

The Prophetic Witness Continues in the New Testament

6. *The Word of God is so completely spoken in Jesus that it is hard to imagine a need for prophets after him. Yet, that Word of God must continue to be shared with those who have not heard. Read Jesus' words to the apostles in* ***Acts 1:8,*** *just before his ascension. What does he say, and how might his words be seen as a continuation of what we have seen in the prophets of the Old Testament?*

   In Acts, Jesus says the Holy Spirit will come upon the apostles, who will thereby receive power to become his witnesses to those around them and throughout the world. As God has given words to the Old Testament prophets and empowered them by the Holy Spirit to proclaim those words to those around them, now God gives the apostles his indwelling presence and power to bear witness to the Word they have all received.

7. ***Reviewing the Context:*** *In Jeremiah 31, we see that God promises to make a New Covenant with his people in which his law will be written on their hearts and minds so they can know him. It is not clear how this will happen. A clue comes in Ezekiel 37, where we see his vision of the dry bones springing to life under the power of the Spirit of God. The prophet Joel (who we do not study in this program) makes a similar prophecy regarding the Spirit that will come about "in those days and at that time" (Joel 3:1; NAB: Joel 4:1).*

   a. *Read* ***Joel 2:28-29*** *(NAB: 3:1-2). According to this, what will be the result of this awaited outpouring of the Spirit, and on whom will it fall?*

      God's Spirit will be poured out on all people, regardless of age, sex, or social status. As a result, the people (not only specific prophets) will dream, have visions, and prophesy. Like the valley of bones coming to life, this illustrates the life that will one day fill all God's people, not just those he has chosen at particular times for special purposes (which was the Old Testament pattern).

   b. *Now read* ***Acts 2:1-18.*** *What happens in the early days after Christ's resurrection and ascension that shows this time has come?*

      The Holy Spirit rushes down upon the disciples in tongues of fire, filling them all and moving them to speak in various languages. Some think they are drunk, but Peter explains it as the fulfillment of Joel's prophecy. The presence of God dwells in the believers (not just in the Temple) through the power of the Spirit, which is the force and power of the Church.

---

[3] Abraham J. Heschel, *The Prophets* (New York: HarperCollins, 1962), xviii, xxix.

8. ***Think About It:*** *Note how the following passages reflect the continuation of the prophetic witness in the early days of the Church.*

   Acts 8:25: The apostles (on whom the Spirit is poured in Acts 7, as promised by Jesus in Acts 1 when he told them to be witnesses) "[speak] the word of the Lord" as they preach.

   Acts 8:34-35: Philip interprets the words of the prophets by "opening his mouth" and telling the Good News of the gospel.

   Acts 15:22-27: To convey the official decision of the Council of Jerusalem, Judas and Silas were specially commissioned to share this teaching in person.

9. *In addition to the type of prophetic witness described above, St. Paul speaks of a "spiritual gift" of prophecy that is given to some.*

   a. *Read* **1 Corinthians 14:1-4.** *What does Paul say about prophecy's desirability and function in the Church?*

      The gift of prophecy is something to be "earnestly" and particularly desired because it builds up, encourages, and consoles people, edifying the Church.

   b. *Note some of the ways in which the gift of prophecy is manifested.*

      Acts 11:27-28: Prophecy can mean foretelling something that will happen in the future, as Agabus foretold a famine so they were able to send relief.

      Acts 15:32: Prophecy can mean exhorting and strengthening other Christians verbally, as Judas and Silas did in the church at Antioch.

   c. *Read* **CCC 799–801.** *What else do you learn about charisms there?*

      Charisms are directed toward the building up of the Church, both to the good of people in general and also to the good of the whole world. It is necessary to discern them carefully and remember that they all are subject to the leadership ("shepherds") of the Church, so that they might work together for the common good. Those charisms that are used in keeping with charity and the true promptings of the Holy Spirit provide a wonderful, rich grace to the Church and its members.

Prophetic Witness in the Church Today

10. *We have seen how the Old Testament prophets foreshadow the ultimate Prophet, Jesus Christ, who has been made "priest, prophet, and king" by God. Every Christian participates by virtue of baptism in these three offices.*[4] *According to CCC 905, what is one way lay people fulfill their prophetic mission?*

    Already anointed at baptism, we do not require a special anointing to "be a prophet." We fulfill that mission in the everyday circumstances of our lives by proclaiming and living according to the Word who is Christ. Neither element is sufficient on its own: Both words and actions are part of the witness, and one who is truly following Jesus will look for occasions to speak and to act accordingly for the benefit of believers and unbelievers alike.

---

4 See CCC 783, 904.

11. *The Church has given us beautiful guidance as we seek to live our share of Christ's prophetic office. Consider the paragraphs from* Lumen Gentium, *the Second Vatican Council's document on the Church, quoted on page 98.*

    In what specific ways can we spread his witness? List three ways that stand out to you from these paragraphs in Lumen Gentium.

Facilitators: Encourage group members to explain why they chose the things they did. *Lumen Gentium* suggests a number of ways to spread his witness. Comments might include some of the following: by living a life of faith and charity; by offering praise; by teaching the Faith; by explaining the Faith and living it out in our families and in the world; by keeping eternity in mind, putting hope in God's promises, and making the most of the present in light of the world to come; by a continual conversion that is not hidden but that is evident to all; by wrestling against evil in our lives in all the forms in which it presents itself.

D. Application

Facilitators: If time allows, have group members share their responses to the following application question.

Read the paragraphs from Lumen Gentium *on page 98 again. Ask the Lord to show you one area in which you could improve your own witness to faith in him. What is it? Think of one thing you can do this week to better live out your prophetic calling, and commit to doing it. If you are afraid or reluctant: What have you learned from your study of the Old Testament prophets that provides courage or strength?*

After the small-group discussion, watch Thomas Smith's video presentation on *Session 10* – New Testament and Modern Prophets: Messengers of the New Covenant.

What's Next?

Get Started by Getting the Big Picture!

Unlocking the Mystery of the Bible

By Jeff Cavins and Sarah Christmyer

Visit BibleStudyForCatholics.com

- Find a *Great Adventure* study in your area.
- Learn how to start a Bible study.
- Join Jeff Cavins and other great Bible teachers for inspiring videos, articles, and study resources.

Questions?

Speak to a friendly and experienced Study Consultant:

call **1-800-376-0520** or visit **AscensionPress.com**

Then …
Dive into Scripture with
The Great Adventure Foundational Series

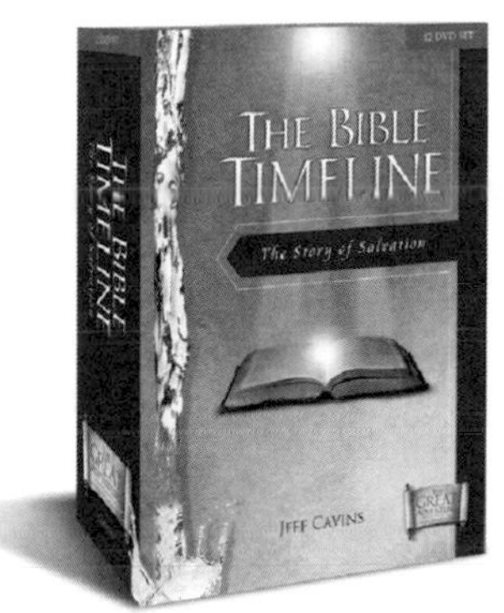

Step 1
The Bible Timeline: The Story of Salvation

Step 2
Matthew: The King and His Kingdom

Step 3
Acts: The Spread of the Kingdom

Continue the Journey

Exodus

Psalms

The Prophets

First Corinthians

Galatians

James

Revelation

Mary

The Mass

Life Application

Catholic Bible Study Resources

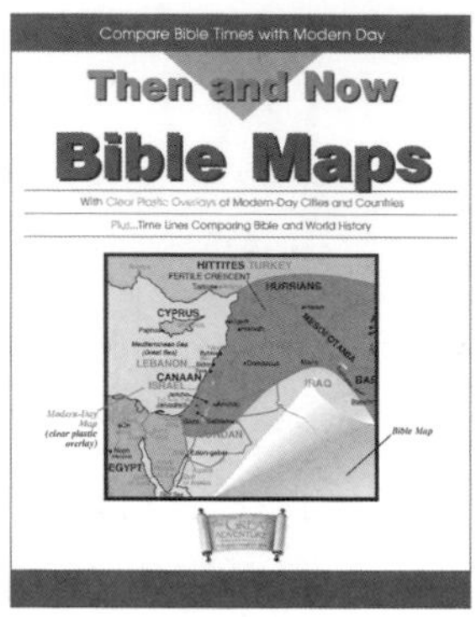

Then and Now Maps

The clear plastic overlays on these full-color maps allow you to compare the places mentioned in the Bible with modern-day cities.

20 pages - spiral bound - 8 ½ x 11

The Bible Thumper; Volumes. 1 & 2

A mini-concordance Bible verse finder with more than 1,000 easy-to-access verses to help Catholics locate and explain the basic teachings of the Faith. Each volume folds out to 33 inches and fits inside most Bibles.

Great Adventure Catholic Bible Indexing Tabs

These pre-cut, one-inch, self-adhesive tabs fit the pages of any full-size Bible and are a great way to help you quickly locate each book of the Bible.

Walking With God: A Journey Through the Bible

by Tim Gray and Jeff Cavins

This captivating and inspirational book follows the central story woven throughout Scripture to reveal God's glorious plan of salvation.

296 pages

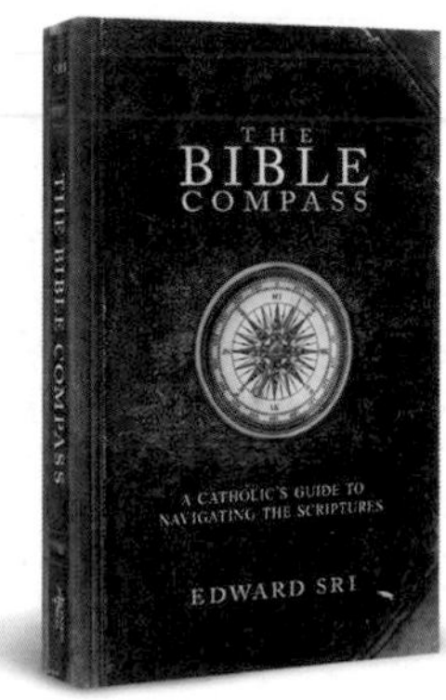

The Bible Compass: A Catholic's Guide to Navigating the Scriptures

by Edward Sri

Get the tools to study the Word of God with confidence, purpose, and in the appropriate context. This book demonstrates how to read the Bible within the living Tradition of the Catholic Church and addresses a host of common questions about the Bible.

174 pages

The Bible Timeline Guided Journal

by Sarah Christmyer

This is more than just a journal; it is a personal guide through the story of salvation history that will help you read the fourteen narrative books of the Bible. The journal includes room for notes as well as thought-provoking questions and tips on how to study the Bible.

236 pages

Praying Scripture for a Change: An Introduction to Lectio Divina

by Tim Gray

flyou are looking for a way to get the most out of prayer, this book is indispensable. Theologian and biblical scholar Dr. Tim Gray walks you through the Bible and teaches you the simple steps of *lectio divina,* a practical and effective way to enhance your prayer life.

Book, 144 pages
Study Guide, 32 pages

Call **1-800-376-0520** or visit **AscensionPress.com**